T0365522

Sher Gill
The Living Master of "The Way to God"

OH MY GOD

I AM THE WAY AND THE WAY IS WITHIN

SHER GILL

authorHOUSE®

AuthorHouse™ UK
1663 Liberty Drive
Bloomington, IN 47403 USA
www.authorhouse.co.uk
Phone: 0800.197.4150

Published by AuthorHouse 05/14/2019

ISBN: 978-1-7283-8104-6 (sc)
ISBN: 978-1-7283-8105-3 (hc)
ISBN: 978-1-7283-8103-9 (e)

For more information about the author and the book, you may visit author's website www.shergill.uk.com or email him at beingasaint@gmail.com.

This Book is Dedicated

To all

Spiritual Seekers

CONTENTS

INTRODUCTION

Where is God? It is everywhere in the State of Consciousness within each individual soul for us to experience and feel God's presence. I have expressed in my writings that every person can make the journey within, and God is waiting for you. God has infinite qualities and is beyond our knowing, but if you manage to experience one glimpse of God in your life, then you can consider yourself lucky and your journey has been worthwhile. I consider myself born lucky because I have been in the presence of God since I was child.

I have seen and lived in the presence of God beyond anyone's expectations or knowing. When I was in the presence of God in march 2008, I was told to express its presence in 250 chapters. God is like a holy tree which has so many branches, and each chapter is an individual branch of this holy tree and expresses God's knowledge or its qualities for us to experience. To me, it was a huge task, and I asked this question within: How is it possible for me to write 250 qualities of God?

To write about one quality of God is difficult, and I am not a professional writer. An answer came. "All you have to do is to hold a pen in your hand, and Spirit will do the writing." That was a big relief.

This is our fifth book, and so far, we have managed to write approximately two hundred branches of this holy tree. In this book there are forty chapters, and each expresses God knowledge and answers many questions. The first chapter is called, "God: Who Am I?" It is based on how man-made religions mislead the followers and fail to express how to experience God's presence in this lifetime. Religions today don't believe in having a living Master.

This is why they fail to understand the true content of its spiritual writings. The living Master can explain the true contents of any spiritual writing and guide the Seeker to go within in the presence of God. The living Master does not rely on any spiritual works written by someone else. God has invested more than enough spiritual knowledge within this individual, and he can write his own holy books. I remember asking this question to Spirit many years ago, knowing that I don't have any holy book which I could claim as my own.

The answer came: "You will write your own." When the flow of Spirit comes, I hold the pen in my hand, and Spirit does the writing. Each chapter leads the Seeker closer to God. May you enjoy reading and making your life worthwhile. The present moment is the king maker. It Just is. Every is-ness is like a drop of rain which disappears into sand without a trace while you are watching. So, make the most of your present life because each moment will lead you in the presence of God if used wisely.

GOD: "WHO AM I?"

I Am The Way, and The Way Is Within. To reach me, it is so simple. Once you make up your mind, sit down and chant, *"Haiome,"* which means, "I will meet you." It also means, "I am here to meet you. Soul knows its way home." In Anami, we were one. Since religions came in, now you are far. I am, was, and will be here, waiting for you like a father waiting for his lost son. Listen to the voice within. The vehicle is sound. The light will show the way.

When you are here, you will know, feel, and ask within, "Have I been away, or was it just a dream?" The lower worlds were only foreign land. It was only an experience. But those souls who are still on the physical plane think I am far away. You now I am as close as your heartbeat. One day, all will know I am here. So, are you in the kingdom of bliss? Since religions came, man's direction of search has changed. I am waiting for them, and they are worshiping idols.

Then a question arises. "Who am I?" All religions agree there is only one God. I am the creator of all creation, but no one approaches me. You have created the riddle, but I show you the way is within. You might fail to reach me, but many have succeeded, and so can you. I am not beyond knowing or unreachable. Follow my spiritual man on earth. He will never fail you. The riddle is this: I exist beyond time and space; therefore, it is difficult to see me. But at the same time, I have given you the capability of travelling beyond time and space to visit me.

Your mind does not let you go because it is the lover of illusion, which is temporary, and it is created for purpose. What is seen visibly is illusion, and what is unseen is eternal. A pilgrimage is not to the temples for my search. It is the journey within, where I am waiting for all my creation. I have created the riddle to amuse the minds. It is similar to the maze: you go in circles and end up coming back to the same point, because all the paths seem the same.

I am so close yet so far at times. All spiritual planes are at a far distance, yet they are within each individual soul and are within your reach. The day you solve this riddle, I will be close to your heart, and you will say, "I know, God." You travel thousands of miles to look for me in temples. "Do you think you will find me there? No, I do not live there or trapped within four walls. I am everywhere. Those who try to erase my name are those who have turned their backs on me.

They are looking for me but in the wrong places. I am residing within each individual soul. This is why you cannot see me. Try to feel my presence as you walk along and feel uplifted spiritually. The time will come when you will know me more. All religions are living in the past and in mythology. I do not live or breathe in the past or in mythology. I am present, if you want to feel my presence. No religious person will come near me, until you come to universal thought via reciting religious verses and acting on them.

All religious people are too busy in their chores, family problems, and praying—not to me but to some pictures of gurus or statues. This is why I do not answer their prayers. I want to listen to their cries, but they do not want me to listen. They are expecting the statues to listen, and I wish they could. This world is full of stones, and some are praying to trees and tying some colourful strings to fulfil their wishes. This world is full of trees. If people are praying to Devi or Devtas (angels) because they believe that they are their Gods, then why should I answer their prayers? I ask, "Who am I?"

I wish they could look for me to simplify their lives, but they prefer to tangle their lives. To this tangled life, some call it enjoyment. They are blinded by illusion, and it has become their God. They cannot see beyond these artificial or temporary needs. The way everyone behaves towards me, I can call everyone Kaffir ("unbelievers") because they have forgotten me completely. The day will come when there will be only one enlightened soul every twelve kilo-meters.

The rest will be sitting in darkness, better known as Kal channels. There are millions of pseudo-masters making billions of dollars, and they are driving the Seekers from the true path. *Pseudo* means they do not know me; otherwise, they would not commit such acts. Only a few have direct faith in me. There are so many sincere and faithful people, but their faith is not in me but in my representatives or prophets. They are taught to have faith in their Masters, who do not even exist in this world.

Their sincerity is also not pure. It is mainly used to fulfil their desires or physical ailments. Out of this sincerity, religions are created, and some temples are created because they believe I only exist in these places. Again, these temples are not in my name. They are privately or publicly owned by organizations. People go to these places to pray or look for me or to feel my presence, although I am living so close in their hearts. I am in each individual soul and everywhere.

When they go to these temples, I wonder where they are going when I am already so close. Now you know why their prayers are not answered. They are depending more on their gurus or teachers. The majority of these teachers don't lead their followers to look for me. Instead, they are telling them to follow their systems or traditional rituals. Any religion having or believing in a caste system, colour, or race of people is not representing me. They are far-far away from my threshold.

If any person, regardless of how religious he may claim to be, acts as Master and others are his servants, then he is not representing me. Each soul is individual, and I have given the capability to all if they want to know me and feel my presence. I am also residing within that servant of yours and in that position. If you feel I am inferior, then how can you know me?

As God: "Who am I?

All objects in the universe and all infinite knowledge put together know what I am. I sent all souls into the lower worlds to unfold and have awareness of me. They are to learn and attain all the qualities, as I do. The challenge is huge, and the mind dictates in the lower worlds, and to know all this is not to mind likings. Overall, every individual feels I am beyond knowing and out of reach, and so I am labelled unknown.

I am like a good father who is humble, who is sincere to all his children, and who provides for all their needs but never has been appreciated. When a negative force (Kal) gives you less and robs you of more, it still shines in your eyes. The known has become the unknown. You make me wonder if I am in the foreign land. This is why questions such as these are often asked: Does God exist? Where is God? Has anyone seen God?

The answers are often in silence or silenced by rude remarks or attacks. This is why new or modern thoughts are arising in this world and say, "I only believe in science or myself (ego)." Religions have failed to represent me in the true image. There is always one person or Master representing me and many others throughout this world who also feel my presence. Instead of learning the spiritual way into my arms, you create religions in their names (prophets), and I am pushed to the side.

All religions celebrate their saints' or prophets' history, such as their births and deaths that happened long ago. During these celebrations, your thoughts travel centuries back, and you dwell in that experience while relating to your guru, whether it was good or bad. But at the present time, you all leave me while claiming that you are searching for me. Can you imagine if people sit in a bus and leave me at a bus stop as they go to see me?

Looking at these situations, question arises within, including this: *Who am I?* I am forgotten by all within my own house. Satnam Ji is my only one true representative; the rest of them are my messengers. This is why they only express part of me. That is why there are so many religions. If all my messengers know me as Satnam does, their message would be same, and there would have been only one religion. The difference in message is the cause of all religious fights.

All religions claim that their guru or teacher is a prophet, but they never wonder if their prophet was involved in any religious wars. At those times, he was not representing me, so how can he be a prophet? My true messenger is often silent or made silent by others because no one is ready to listen or face the truth. Those who are converting others religiously are against spiritual law. They believe that they are doing my will, but they are wrong because I did not create any religions.

All religions are man-made and established for many reasons. Conversion is a clear indication of creating bad karma. Those who are fighting religious wars are also against my wishes. There is no religion that did not fight a religious war, and so all these religions are not representing me or their prophets. Those who kill in the name of religion are going far from me and are losing my love. Now it is a known factor: those who kill in the name of religion are not religious.

Even their own people are saying this and condemning these acts. They are also aware that they are killing in the name of religion, but in effect they are executing their own anger due to their own negative experiences in life. Those religious leaders or prophets who are killing my creation or are recommending that killing and eating of animals is normal, cannot represent me. I am responsible to feed the whole creation. Then how can I or my representatives recommend you to eat meat?

When a person is suffering and has given up on his or her religion, which often fails the individual, then religious leaders stress having stronger faith rather than helping the individual. As Jesus said once, man shall not live by bread alone. Why does this person not get any help? Because they are all dead religions. Their Masters or gurus do not exist anymore.

The day will come when no one will answer your prayers, and you will cry in vain and make a request: "Whoever you are and wherever you are, please help me." I will answer and help because you are part of myself. I am responsible for all; your sufferings are my own because I experience your sufferings myself. I have always helped, but I want you to become aware of everything consciously. At last, this person who has given up comes to one conclusion and says, "Wherever you are, please help me, God."

Only then does this person come in contact with my live channel, or I appear in disguise. People often fail to feel my presence because they want to see me under their conditions. If you arise above your conditions, needs, and thoughts, I am always here. My whole creation is having problems due to their own created bad karma, but they often raise their hands in the air, pointing at me and asking for help. Did you ever think, "If I have problems, to whom do I complain?" I like to see everyone take responsibility for their own actions and let me be as I am, just as I let you be yourself.

In the future, spiritual science (spiritual travel) is the only hope. It means the practical side of God bringing back the souls to me. This spiritual science will prove all the religions are fake and baseless and have no practical answer to any question. Eventually, people will lose their faith and walk away to practical spiritual science in order to experience my presence and directly. All the known prophets and their names will become unknown, as I am at present.

God: "Who am I?

6

EYE OF SOUL

When the spiritual Seeker is searching for the truth, spiritual freedom, or any esoteric experiences, then a number of statements are given by religions or cults to attract the Seeker. The biggest attraction is spiritual travel (the soul), followed by Divine Light and Sound, past lives, telepathy, and miracles—the list is endless. What will be or are the main points or virtues we need to look at for our success or failure? Yet we expect to do spiritual travel.

"What is this point we need to look at?" That is our first eye, which is often known as the "Third-Eye". The soul is here for schooling on the physical plane to experience. "Where is the seat of soul in the physical body?" Two eyes are for our physical use, and most of the illusion is seen or experienced through them. They are the main cause for creating our karma. We often blame the mind for our wrong-doings, but don't forget that our two eyes first saw something, and then mind executed the situation, either to create good or bad karma in our account.

The result is based on what our two eyes have seen. It is also important to know which mind was active at that time, the lower or spiritual. "Where is our first eye which is responsible for spiritual travel and other esoteric experiences?" That is our Pineal Gland, which is known as the Seat of the soul. Although it is a physical organ in the head, at the same time it is one of the most important spiritual centre. To our physical knowledge, it is known as the third eye because we only heard of it through some religious scriptures or mythological stories.

At present, it is beyond our knowledge or out of reach. Once you come to know the third eye's presence, then you will prefer to view this world and beyond through this eye. Now you know why it is our first eye. When you are in meditation or are asking Spirit for answers to your problems, they are given through this spiritual centre and passed over to the mind and further on to astral body to express the result in the physical regarding your wishes.

How many of you are paying any attention to the pineal gland's welfare when there are so many? Half of you don't even know, where it is in the head, and yet you believe to be serious spiritual Seekers. When you want to learn any subject, you have to learn from scratch to finish, mastering the subject. All professional sports-people condition their bodies to perform at the competition. Although we are not competing with anyone, our competition is within. So, what are you doing to condition yourself to accomplish your spiritual goal?

When T. E. Lawrence went to join the Great Arab Revolt as a liaison officer in 1916, he made a thorough study of that country and the nature of people and the possible problems he was going to face. He only felt comfortable to take this task until he realised fully what he was going to be involved with. At the end, he was very successful. In the same way, we have to study thoroughly the subject of soul, spiritual centres, and the welfares of them.

Every person in this world knows or has heard of the word *soul*, but simply knowing these four letters is not going to lead you anywhere. There are two basic welfares of the pineal gland to look into, physical and spiritual. For the physical, if the pineal gland is not healthy, it affects the physical body, and some symptoms will indicate this. Medical experts are aware of this, and it is very important to eat healthy foods to activate the pineal gland.

Vegetarian food makes a lot of difference. Vegetarian food is mainly water based, and so it is considered clean and healthy with high vibrations. It helps to keep the pineal gland healthy. Seaweed kelp found in the ocean has many nutrients (such as iodine), and it is very good for the pineal gland. Seaweed kelp also helps to fight cancer. Kelp is available in most health stores. Animals drink water, and they do have blood in their bodies similar to humans.

That is where the difference comes in between vegetarian and non-vegetarian foods. Because animals have blood in their bodies, do you know they have their own individual DNA? Vegetarian food is water based, and or its DNA is in our favour. Now, can you imagine the number of DNA you added to your body within one life span? The stronger the DNA, the more you add karma to your account. After adding so much DNA to your account, surely you can imagine how healthy your spiritual side is.

I don't think your pineal gland is as active as you want to see or expect it to be. This is the answer to those who ask, "What difference does it make?" The pineal gland is the seat of the soul or the third eye. It should be active and healthy. Spiritual travel is only possible if the pineal gland is healthy. If it is not healthy, it is not going to stir the positive vibrations that we need before any spiritual travel is possible. If physically it is healthy, then we have to tune it spiritually in order to keep it active all the time.

Tuning yourself spiritually is very important to materialise your goal. There are many ways you can do this. Do your spiritual exercises regularly, have total reliance on your spiritual Master, read discourses or given spiritual material in the shape of books, and mentally fast. You must keep your pineal gland active so that you can do spiritual travel any time. To those who fail in this experience, you expect to do spiritual travel during meditation.

But the question is, have you prepared yourself for this experience, or did you assume it is going to happen because you want it to happen?

Other signs of an unhealthy pineal gland are that you will not have good, clear dreams, or you will not remember them. This may be the answer to those who are complaining about this issue. It may not be correct if I say the Master gives you the spiritual dreams but doesn't want you to remember them.

If he doesn't want you to remember them, then what is the purpose of giving them to you in the first place? Our book *The Will of God* is the result of remembering all the dreams because they are given for a purpose. In very rare cases, the Master gives you the experience and only gives you a nudge that something has taken place. It is always for the benefit of the Seeker. The examples given above are good for keeping your pineal gland decalcified, and they will activate the gland.

The pineal gland is calcified when there is a lot of toxic material built around it; as explained earlier, non-vegetarian food is not good for it. We must eat natural foods to remove this build-up of crystallised deposits around it. Many people prefer to drink lots of water. Do you know it brings lots of fluoride, chlorine, and bromide? They all contribute to calcifying your pineal gland unless you have a water purifier system installed in your household or drink bottled water.

The majority of the foods we eat are genetically modified. They are not natural as we believe, and they all contribute to toxifying this gland and are a cause for cancer in the human body. Try to purchase organic foods if possible. Other foods toxic to this gland are sugar, caffeine, alcohol, cocaine, and heroin. Smoking is the worst. We know it is toxic for our lungs and leads to cancer, but it is also bad for the pineal gland. Neem leaves extract from Indian trees is very good for decalcifying.

Too many headaches and heavy heads after waking up from sleep are signs of a toxic presence. If you wake up happy and feel light-headed, that is a sign of good health. We never pay much attention to our heads apart from washing our faces, shaving, or putting on make-up (which covers your true expression of soul). If our skulls and other organs, which are too many to name, are healthy, then who needs make-up? The appearance of getting old, which normally we see on everyone's face, is the result of what is going on within our skulls.

The whole body depends on the head. When we fail to sleep, there is something going on within, making us feel uncomfortable, and our nervous system is also not in harmony. This is why good, healthy foods and keeping spiritual vibrations high are very important to spending our lives in a balanced and happy manner. There is one experience we all have now and then. We feel a nice, warm sensation within the forehead area.

This happens during meditation, or sometimes it happens when we have positive thoughts during the day. It is good to have, but we need to go further. Due to spiritual efforts, the Third-Eye becomes active, which is the seat of soul. This activation shows our spiritual vibrations are being stirred within the skull area, but we fail to go any further. If you sit down, take advantage of this activation, and try to concentrate on the pineal gland where the soul is sitting down calmly.

Once you can feel its presence, then action is required to move the soul through the Crown-Chakra. Spiritual travel is not easy, as we expect it to be, but experience given by the spiritual Master is very easy. It is very similar to a toy given to the child. This child is very happy, but this child did not go to work to earn money so this child could buy this toy with his or her own effort. It is same when you buy things with your pocket money that you did not earn either. Now you see if you want to do something at your own accord, it is not that easy.

It is same as when we use this phrase very often: "You need to become the Master of your own universe." These are very attractive words, but this is how you have to materialise with your efforts. You probably now realise, when you read about successful yogis and saints, they live on less and eat natural foods. They are in meditation most of the time, either sitting down in tailor fashion or mentally fasting when walking.

I can write a lot more on this subject, but now the question is, "Is your Eye of soul healthy, and do you know where it is? Are you trying to find its existence? If you do, are you using your first eye properly to do spiritual travel? You know it is not your third eye; to the spiritual people, it is their first eye. To the others who are unaware, it is their third eye. The pineal gland is also known as the mystery gland because this is the way to reach higher levels of consciousness, while still being present in the physical body.

The pituitary gland is the seat of mind, and it is also known as the master gland. It is situated behind the bridge of nose and below the base of brain, and it is very close to the optic nerve. It controls other hormone glands such as the adrenal and the thyroid. It is usually pea size and weighs about 0.5 grammes. It is situated within a small bone cavity. It is responsible for regulating a number of functions in balance.

1. Body over or undergrown in size is due to the malfunction of the pituitary gland.
2. Blood pressure.
3. Balance of water within body.
4. Energy.
5. Sex organs.
6. Temperature regulation.

The recommended vitamins for the pituitary gland are A, D, and E.

A tumour on the pituitary gland can be responsible for headaches, fatigue, and more symptoms. Vitamin E prevents oxidative damage to the pituitary gland.

The thyroid gland is situated in the neck area and is responsible for controlling our growth and metabolism. Two small adrenal glands sit on top of the kidneys and help us deal with our stress by releasing the hormones. As said earlier, the pituitary gland is responsible for controlling the hormones in certain glands. Now you see how important it is to look after the pituitary gland as well.

Now I am going to attach one sketch which shows very clearly and exactly where your pituitary and pineal glands are. Study them thoroughly to see. Have you been putting your attention in the correct place all these years? Although the pineal gland is the seat of soul or the third eye, and the pituitary gland is the seat of the mind, if you manage to stir the vibrations on either gland, the whole area within the dots becomes live. You will feel the sensation within your forehead area, and the strength of your attention will indicate your success of experience.

Such as sensation only, seeing light, hearing sound, deep samadhi, and finally an out-of-body experience. I am sure this chapter has given you some insight of the spiritual glands in order to keep them healthy— and most important, how to use them. Every soul has the right to see through this eye. We often hear statements such as, "What is reality?" Reality is only experienced through the eye of the soul, when it is open. Truth witnessed through two physical eyes is only world knowledge. Will you have success?

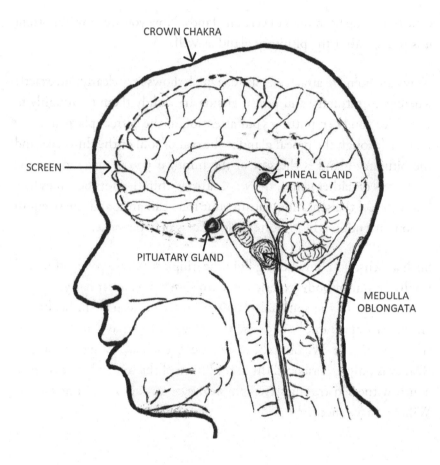

This sketch has been drawn over a real X-ray taken at a hospital to show the position of the pineal and pituitary glands. I have already given pictures of these glands in my book "The Way to God" to appear simple to understand. These are 100 percent correct positions, so you can master your technique to materialise a successful experience. If you find it difficult to locate them, please use your imagination to believe that you are focusing on them. Successful imagination can help stir the vibrations.

A forehead screen is mainly used to visualise the picture of the spiritual Master. When we recommend you, to pull attention backwards from the screen, it is because of the position of these glands; otherwise, most of your effort is wasted. A successful stir of vibrations can turn the whole dotted area near the third eye, very similar to a light in a room. Once this dotted area is spiritually enlightened, then focus on the screen. That can lead you to see the light and attention centred in the middle area (inner ears), which can lead you to hear the sound.

Feeling the presence of soul and gently looking up can lead the soul through the crown chakra and a successful spiritual travel. There is one more point to be noted from the sketch: the crown chakra is not exactly on top of the pineal gland. This is why I ask you to lift your chin slightly up; only then can the crown chakra, pineal gland, and the backbone appear in one straight line to have successful flow of Spirit.

Make the effort, and you will have success.

—

ART OF LIVING

You have to be an artful dodger to survive in this world. The whole world has lost this art and suffers at the hands of each other. God did not create our lives to suffer as much as we are doing. We must learn to live stress-free. What is the main cause for stress? We have forgotten how to love each other and give impersonal love to all of God's creation. This whole world has become a royal rumble, and everybody is fighting for the individual.

A famous religious verse, "Good of the whole", is forgotten or practiced half-heartedly. Unless we have stress-free minds and a violence-free society, we cannot have peace because under the conditions we are living, there is some kind of fear ticking within ourselves. Our main cause of suffering is that we have forgotten how to fight like ultimate warriors, which means we are depending on too many people and our self-confidence is very low.

Build up your stamina in such a way that you are strong enough to face the whole world alone. You should feel that you are the best ever born on this earth. When you lose your confidence, the reasons are many: personality conflict, financial status, education, and body strength. Once you begin to feel inferior to others, your suffering begins, and life becomes miserable. Taking responsibility in life is very important. If you are responsible in all actions taken, then most of the things or problems will fade away.

Do not expect happiness all the time; life is a mix of happiness and sadness. Do not try to be too happy on happy occasions or too sad in sad moments. Learn to live a balanced life; that way you can avoid many hurting moments. Those who live in balance never fail in life. Those who have a habit of living happily often get hurt very quickly when dramatic situations take place in life. In marriage, people often get hurt because things are not working according to your expectations.

Every single person lives in a self-created world, and in order to live happily, we must learn tolerance because everyone have the right to express their opinion. We must learn to accept people as they are; things only go out of proportion, when we want the things to happen our way. Others' way of life could be better than yours, if you have the patience and examine it thoroughly. At or before marriage, we all have fairy-tale imaginations about our partners: handsome, kind, loving, etcetera.

But you never know what your fate has in store for you. It is possible that your world could turn upside down and a non-stop battle has begun. With patience and love, all this can calm down, but our frustration exploits everything out of proportion. Up to our wedding day, it is our glorious moments, and after that it all becomes stress and hardships. If we create love and affection for each other, the magic in life returns. Keep that passion alive, the one you had when you met first time.

Life will bring very surprising moments as it unfolds, and the butterflies are still around, the colourful ones you had seen earlier. Keep working on building that trust for each other. Broken trust is the killer of relationships. In marriage or a friendly circle, we all should make an effort to build relationships. One-sided effort in any situation is not healthy, and with time everything will vanish, whether someone is a friend or in love. In one-sided friendship or love, we often get hurt.

No one has won the world with violence. Love is winner all the time. We always look for compatibility in love or friendship because this is what we have learned from our families or society. If two people are too compatible, two things can happen. They can be very successful and make themselves very big in life, or the things can happen in the opposite way because both loves to express their opinions but do not tolerate what has been said by the other, bringing catastrophic results.

We must learn to give psychic space to each other. In marriage we are tagged as husband or wife, and domination takes place. It is better to live life as very good friends, and during hard times we stand with each other like solid rocks. Hardship and happiness are part of our lives. We must learn to move on in life as we progress with time; we all are in constant change. Don't hold on to the past that is history.

I have heard many times from couples saying, "He is not the same man I married," or, "She is not as pretty as she used to be." With time and responsibility, we all change. We cannot remain twenty-five forever, and old age takes its toll. Mistakes of the past should not be repeated—that kills the relationship. No one is perfect in this world. During some quarrel, Jesus Christ said to the crowd, "Any person who has not committed any sin should throw the stone first," and everyone stepped back.

This is the truth. People who are simple in minds and live simple lives are the most-happier because they have very few demands and have nothing to gain or lose. I always believed in looking good and feeling better and people around you can see the spark in your personality. People often ignore those who are miserable or looking dull. Your personality can pull people towards you like a magnet; otherwise, everything repels.

Always learn to appreciate what you have, I always believed that before its time or beyond your luck, you will not receive, and nothing will come your way. Be satisfied with what you have. We often fail when we begin to dream that the grass is greener in the next field. We often end up making mistakes and losing what we have. Those people who are allegedly looking better than you, are often suffering in silence without giving away any hint to anyone.

You will find lots of brown spots in their grass. It does not matter where you go; many grasses have bald patches as well. As you do your religious prayers at dinner or suppertime, be grateful for what you have. You often have a rat race in life, trying to get rich or get good status in life, being better than the people you know. This also brings misery when you don't succeed. Negative attitude makes a big hole in your aura or persona, things begin to fade away, and you end up losing what you already had.

My approach to life is different. What God has given me already is above average, I am not super rich or poor, so why should I complain? Be satisfied with what you have, and you will always be happy. You can find happiness in a flower. Otherwise, millions of pounds cannot make you happy. Every person is a hero in his or her own way. You have the confidence, and God has given you common sense. Be in command of your life. We fail only when someone else is pulling our strings and bring misery into our lives.

There are people who will be jealous in many ways and try to harm you, and in return you may hold grudges. This could be a silent killer because it will affect your mind and health. Learn to forgive and leave them alone. If you don't retaliate, they will move somewhere else to feed their negative habit. Keep yourself happy within, and you will never grow old; wrinkles on your face are the result of stress. Honesty is the key to a happy and healthy life.

Wherever you are working, be honest with the task you have been given and do enough work to earn your living. Never forget that someone is paying you for each minute, hour, or day. Live your life actively and honestly. Laziness is responsible for poor health and stress. Doing physical exercises eliminates lots of illnesses and side effect ailments. A few minutes of exercise can save your day. Live your day in such a way that it is your last day in this world and you are going to make the most of it.

Respect and appreciate all life; in return, you will get abundance of love. We all are social creatures, and if you are not strong enough to live alone, then have a circle of friends who will be there when you need them. Help others as much as you can because it will give you pleasure. No one is perfect. Do not try to find faults in others. Self-analysis is important because it could be you at fault. Have a special goal in life apart from your normal work or family.

So that at the end of your life, you can say to yourself, "Yes, I have achieved this." Otherwise, you will be a person like any other in the world who came and went without a trace. Make your mark in this world. Keep moving towards your set goal and be focused. Failures will be many, but never give up. It is this hunger within that keeps you alive and strong. God sent souls on earth to learn. The physical body is given to express itself and execute its actions of learning, so learn as much as you can.

Keep moving, and with time you will mature. We cannot remain children all our lives. Moving and travelling is important. You cannot know the whole world standing in one place or living in the same house. The whole world is waiting for you to be explored. Taking risk in life is important because it will build your stamina and self-confidence. Otherwise, life is slipping through your fingers every day. We often fail ourselves by saying, "I can't do this."

There will be so many who want to see you fail in life. However, we often fail ourselves. Time is very important and every minute counts, so don't sleep like junk on the heap—make the most of your day. Then you can say, "Today, I have done this or that." Life is to be lived like an example to the others. Dive into the sea of life to find pearls. Hold lots of love within until you become the magnet of love. Then you don't need to find love because everyone will be attracted to you, and the choice will be yours.

Don't search for love—be the creator of love. You can bring magic in many people lives. Divorce is only for those people who are dominating, non-tolerant, and bored easily or unserious in life. Hold on to the little smile on your face because it can make someone else's day. If you suspect something is wrong, learn to say no; otherwise, it can bring lots of misery in your life later. You don't have to drag your life when you can run on roller skates.

Don't feel empty in life. Fill each corner of your life to experience and let people feel awe, saying, "How did you do it?" If you have committed a mistake somewhere in life, undo the situation if you can, or at least learn to say sorry. All mental pressure will be released. Sometimes it is better to have or make a blunt statement now rather than telling hundreds of lies later. Never expect rewards for your good deeds; it can lead to depression.

A person who was suffering from depression went to see a doctor. The doctor gave him a number of medicines and recommended a few other therapies, but nothing worked. At the end, he suggested to this patient, watch a very famous circus in that area. The joker of this circus was very famous for making people laugh. The doctor was sure it should work. This patient replied, "I am that joker."

Then the doctor asked this patient, "In your opinion, who do you think is the biggest joker in this world?" The patient pointed his thumb up towards the sky, meaning God.

God is responsible for the whole creation, and it is very similar to any circus. According to God, it has created everything equal and opposite, in proportion to keep a perfect balance. God thought of each soul's survival and provided all means of living and feeding natural gifts to fight against any disease. The five passions of our minds are driving us in different directions. We are full of greed, ego, and desire to be more powerful than anyone else.

God created this land of happiness, but we are never satisfied because we have been given everything easily and free. This is why we do not appreciate what we have received. The five passions of our minds are deadly when abused, but if they are kept in balance, then the same five passions can bring lots of spices in our lives to enjoy. That is their purpose in the first place. All lower lives are living according to nature and are happy.

Did you ever see any bird or animal going to see the doctor on its own or going to a shopping centre? The answer is no. They follow the dictates of God and are living happily. Mind you, all wildlife receives food on a daily basis without fail. Do you know why? Because they trust the joker within. All domestic pets such as dogs and cats are more likely to get sick than wild ones, and we take them to the veterinarian for treatment to make them feel better.

Do you know why they get sick? Because they are imprisoned within four walls, similar to humans. Be yourself and let the others be. Live your life in the name of God. It will take care of all your needs. Vacuum all materials from life and fill it up with Spirit.

This is the art of living.

⸺

AWAGAVAN WHEEL OF 84

In the beginning, we should know the number of God's creation. According to old Hindu religious texts, there are approximately 3 million plant species and 2.7 million insect species, 1.4 million bird species, 0.9 million sea species and 0.4 million land animals. The total is 8.4 million or 84 lakh incarnations, and above all others are humans, angels, and demons.

As humans, we are always concerned about our well-being. First, we should know what we are. The physical body is known as Pinda or Isthul sharir, which means one day it is bound to die or be destroyed in one way or the other. These words *Pinda* and *Sharir* are from the Hindu language and mean the human body. This Pinda is known as the genetic entity (GE), which is made up of chemicals of nature. It is really an oxygen machine which dies naturally, accidentally, or intentionally. It is used by the soul as a shell for temporary basis during each incarnation.

The process of death in a natural basis is as follows. The soul leaves the body and enters into the next life. The soul usually leaves at the pineal gland and finds its way through the crown chakra, but not always. In the case of a person with a lower consciousness, the soul can leave through any one of psychic chakras. This is the case of most of humankind today.

This has been proven by our medical science that near the time of natural death, numbness begins to creep up the feet area, gradually move higher along the body until it reaches the heart-centre. Then it stopped due to a lack of blood circulation. There is a sensation of some kind, and then the soul is free like a bird to fly or to be escorted by Jam-Dutes. The soul breaks the silver cord with the clay shell it has used for a number of years. No physical pain is experienced.

Any natural death is no more painful than birth. The silver cord is still attached between the astral, causal, mental, and soul body. It is the astral body which is going to represent the soul in the court of Dharam-Raj, not the soul as many believe. It is very similar to the physical body representing us on this plane. Souls with heavy karmic patterns leave through lower chakras of spine instead of the natural means through the third eye.

After death, the only growing thing left is the nails and hairs if the body is kept for a number of days or until it begins to decay. As any human dies naturally, at that particular time, Jam-Dutes or angels of death appear to escort the soul to the astral plane in the court of Dharam-Raj, the king of the dead. He is always in court to take care of all newcomers. There is no waiting or sitting in some jail cell, as described by most religious texts.

After his judgement, he draws the curtain over your past life's memories so that you can accept your new incarnation and its conditions of living as the will of God without questioning. One in a million may remember a past life. Although there are a number of sections to accommodate everyone, there is a waiting period of a minimum of seventy-two hours, or it could be many years if the soul's exact karma does not match for future learning.

All souls do not come back to this earth if the very minimum karma is left. Then they are given a chance to proceed into higher planes. All religions stress that birth in human form is very important. God has gifted the soul with awareness of all other bodies, which actively helps the soul to shed all karma on all planes at once, directly proceed to the soul plane, and achieve spiritual freedom. The process of death is enacted upon every plane, after finishing karma on the physical plane.

Now we are in the astral plane and work out our karma according to that plane. In the same way, the astral body has to be dispersed there and move in the court of the causal plane. There, the causal body will represent the soul for the judgement, and the Dharam-Raj of that plane will decide the future incarnation on the astral plane. Alternatively, you may proceed to the mental plane or the soul plane.

The majority of religious followers are not following their respected religions for many reasons, or they do not take it seriously. It is the fear of death and future consequences in heaven and hell regarding their wrong-doings which is pumped into their brains by the priests. This is the calculated formula of previous saints, who knew that humans are the only creatures of God who are always aggressive towards God's ways. Instead of submitting and adjusting to God's ways, humans always calculate how to outsmart God's ways and getting the best of nature.

People believe, guided by priests that you will be tortured in many ways, or you will be dropped in fire or put in boiling oil. All these statements lead to one conclusion: that you have been punished for your wrong-doings. It also means that now you have become karma-less. If that is the case, then how can you have another incarnation on earth? At the same time, they also point out your coming back to earth for the next incarnation.

They are all contradictory to their own statements because none of them have any practical experience in this field; they simply pass on information heard from somewhere. When people hear the name of Jam-Dutes, it brings fear within all. They do not know who these souls are. Dharam-Raj is the head of this responsibility. Dharam means religion, the person who act as the true righteous of justice, and he do not waver from his true duty. He is also known as Yama.

His assistants are known as Dutes. Dutes means ministers, very similar to our physical parliament. That is why they are called Yam-Dutes, which mean people or angels sent by Dharam-Raj to escort the soul to its court. Therefore, how can they mistreat any person? Death is the beginning of true life in God's worlds. It is known that death is only an illusion, and then there is little need for you to have cause of fear. This fear is only created by priests.

Yama is also known as self-discipline, and there is another interpretation for this: not killing any creation of God and living life as directed by God. This is the death procedure of normal people, but those who follow any true Master or messenger of God are directly escorted by the Master to their earned spiritual plane. The true Master always guides followers to set their minimum goal. It should be Self-Realisation, but you can achieve God-Realisation in this life too.

———

BIG BROTHER IS WATCHING

In life, we try to get away with almost anything we can. This is how we have been trained by our families or society. If not, sometimes circumstances force us to follow the path of deception; as the saying goes, everything is fair in love or war. Most of the people, though they are religious, ignore the ethics of their beliefs. They believe if no one is looking, they can get away with it. First of all, you always know that your actions are negative or positive.

It does not matter if you are aware of your actions or not, but you should know that Big Brother is always watching you. Now you may be wondering, "Who is this Big Brother?" It is God itself, who always gives the nudge within to make you aware of your actions. Second, it is within. You are always aware of your actions, and you can ignore the whole world, but within you cannot over look. This overlooking is the cause of your suffering. It is known as karma.

Once there was a saint. In his old age, he decided to choose his successor from his followers. There were only two deserving ones in his opinion. *He thought, I'd better test them to see who is more sincere to God.* He called both and gave them the same task to follow. The saint handed them one pigeon each and said, "Kill these pigeons where you think no one is looking or watching you. The one who comes back first will be eligible to take my place." Both walked away.

One of them looked around and thought no one was looking, so he broke the neck of his pigeon and killed it. He came back to his teacher. "Saint, I have killed it where no one was watching or looking at us, so I have come back first." For his second disciple, they waited for long time. After a long time, he came back with the live pigeon in his hands. The first disciple was happy and thought he was the winner. The saint asked his second disciple, "How come you did not kill your pigeon?"

The disciple answered, "I went everywhere, and no humans were looking, but God was looking. Then I went inside a dark room so no one could see us, but my inner state of consciousness was looking. This is why it took me so long to return." He realised that Big Brother was watching him everywhere. The saint was pleased with his answer and chose him as his successor. I have two bird feeders in my garden, and it's lovely to see birds eat seeds. Sometimes it is very interesting to watch them.

On average fifty to one hundred parrots turn up daily, and their routine is to sit directly on the birdfeed cage. There are others who only pick up what has been dropped on the ground by parrots. There are a few magpies, sparrows, two robins, two pigeons, and three doves. Squirrels play their own games to steal. There is always a rivalry between pigeons and doves. The pigeons always chase away the doves so they cannot eat whatever is dropped on the ground by parrots.

When pigeons are not around, then there is one dove bigger in size than the other two, and she chases the small doves maybe forty feet away and then she comes back to eat. But all of them have the same aim: to fill up their bellies. It gives me pleasure to watch them, but at the same time I notice their behaviour of cheating and domination. Good luck to them. I do not interfere; it's a law of nature. But at the same time, they are not aware that Big Brother is watching their misdeeds.

In the animal kingdom, there is jungle law. Hunters can claim whatever they spot, grab, and kill. They begin with lions and tigers because they are the strong pack. For example, they manage to kill buffalo. Then a pack of hyenas arrives, and they always come in big numbers. They irritate the lion pack in such a way that the lions leave their kill, and hyenas eat the feast. Now the question arises, who created the karma?

This is what people think, and they say, "We did not kill; we only eat that which was already killed or dead." We follow this in steps. First, the farmer is responsible for raising his animal stock for slaughter purposes only. Second, animals are led to the slaughter machine. Third, the drivers transport meat to the shops or stores. Fourth, butchers at the meat shop cut the meat into small pieces for selling purposes only. Fifth, those who buy the meat, will clean and cook it.

But this last person thinks he is not really responsible. Do not forget that you are the last person to dispose of the animal body by eating it. Did you notice the whole procedure is in five steps? The circle is complete, and none of these five people had any pity on the animals. Now we follow this from a different viewpoint. For whom did the farmer raise his animal stock? For whom was the animal killed? For whom was it transported? For whom was the meat cut into pieces? Who went to the shop willingly to buy meat?

As I said, we humans always have a habit of self-denial of any wrongdoing. If this last person (the customer) was not available, then the whole procedure would have never taken place. So, you don't decide how responsible you are in this act. It is the job of Big Brother, who is always watching you.

No one can deceive Big Brother.

—

BLACK MAGIC

Black magic is one of the deadliest, scariest, and most dangerous occupational hazards in this world. Occupational means these black magicians do not provide this service for free. They are fully trained people, and though many pretend to be black magicians, they are known as pseudo-masters, and many naive people are robbed of their money with no service provided. In Asian countries like India and Pakistan, and in Africa, there is a big demand for these practitioners.

The sad part is, when these people moved into European countries or other parts of the world, this negative practice also travelled with them. The root cause of this practice is jealousy. "Now, the question is who wants to harm you? The people you are very proud of, better known as your own near and dear family. The big population of this world doesn't know, who you are and what you do or don't do; they have no concern. The people who are very close know what you do, and they watch you like a hawk.

If you are poor and suffering, most of them are happy; one or two may be concerned and try to help you. The behaviour of these people is based on their upbringing. This is what they have learned from parents or the society in which they live. For any person who finds success with hard work or becomes successful overnight, I don't think that it is much appreciated in the close circle. They may pretend to congratulate you, but their minds have devious schemes to bring you down from your throne.

When nothing works, they approach black magicians. You may be wondering, how you can find these people. It is so simple. The majority of Asian newspapers are full of adverts by these people. This is why I said earlier that out of these advertisements, some are genuine and many are pseudo. When any person is suffering, he or she is willing to approach anyone who claims to be the practitioner of black magic, and he or she is willing to pay for this service.

What is black magic? It is the use of evil spirits for evil purposes and to harm others. It is considered a dark art because it is used to control or harm others who are irritating your mind in many ways. To this art, people give different names such as black magic, sorcery, witchcraft, occult practice, and more. For those who are influenced by this practice, if they feel that you or someone else is crossing their path, then they will do their best to prevent you from achieving your dream.

Black magic is sent through certain postulates of evil spirits to the person to be harmed. Once you become a black magician there is no turning back. Some charge a small amount of money to earn their living. Others charge a large amount of money. It depends on your reputation. Apart from earnings, you are creating lots of bad karma for yourself at the cost of peoples suffering, caused by your wrong-doing. The person who hired you for this purpose is also bound to suffer.

I don't think both parties are able to pay it back that easily. You may feel happy to see someone suffering at the hands of your wrong-doing, but one day it is all going to back fire on you. I have come across some black magicians throughout the years. At the end of their life span and near death, physically they suffered a lot. The lord of karma makes sure these people suffer, he does not spare anyone, and does not stop anyone from this negative practice.

God has given free will to all souls to live their lives and do as they wish. White magicians aim to help others, undo negative spells, and bring peace and justice to the people who approach them. Black magic is used for many reasons. They use this practice to control someone in love, to communicate with wandering souls after the death of a physical body, or to control someone as a slave. To achieve immortality is their belief, but it cannot be done through negative force.

"I don't think many of these practitioners know what true spiritual freedom is? Black magicians consider the outcome of what their customer wants to see, and there are a number of rituals that can be used for different purposes. Rituals used for controlling someone cannot be used for gaining wealth or talking to the dead, and vice versa. Very rarely do black magicians visit the customer's house to practice, unless there is something in the house which is very disturbing and has to be seen and dealt with there and then.

Normally, black magicians have built a system at their own living place, and all the required equipment is at hand because they use some items to bring the result. They use candles, herbs, crystals, and very expensive perfumes to attract the entities. They also have harmful items such as dolls and needles. These needles are used on dolls to send pain to the person to be harmed while reciting the relevant black magic or spell. They poke needles into the doll, believing that this is the person involved for suffering.

At a successful attempt, this victim will suffer, and distance is no problem. People in India send this kind of wrong-doing to England, Canada, and rest of the world. Sometimes one attempt is enough; otherwise, it is repeated a number of times to get the result for their customers and send the misery to those considered an enemy. The majority of time the victims are innocent, decent, and down-to-earth people, but the way you look at them, they appear to be as your enemy.

Sometimes the black magician or the person who wants to hurt someone gets into trouble as well. If the opposite person is a saint or holds a very high state of consciousness, that aura is formed into a circle and act as a mirror. Whatever is sent to the person often reflects back to the sender, and then the black magician and the customer receives back their own medicine, not knowing how this can be. When using these dark forces, the practitioner must be very careful, fully trained and in control of the situation.

When these forces used naively, these dark forces can backfire on the doer and can become insane. A number of people end up in mental hospitals, and treatment given by normal doctors will not work. A small mantra (magic) can end their misery in minutes or hours. Some people have normal physical disability and believe it is some kind of black magic done by someone. They are innocent people, end up in the wrong hands, and give away their livelihood for no reason.

Despite their efforts, physical ailment still exists. Sometimes when things are not working according to one's plans in life, some people take it as someone placing black magic on them. All the time, it is not true, and sometimes these troubles arrive at your doorstep due to self-created bad karma. All kinds of sufferings are not black magic, and these black magicians are no friends to anyone; they are only interested in your money.

In India, expert black magicians use graveyards to trap new entities. People in India use pyres to burn corpses. The pyre is assembled by stacking some amounts of wooden pieces, the corpse is placed on top, and the ritual is to set fire by their loved ones. It takes a few hours to burn the corpse, and then it takes few hours to cool the ashes or remains of the body. The next day, family members go back to the graveyard and pick up unburned bones, nails, and more.

These black magicians go there at mid-night to pick up the skull if it is fully intact. In the majority of cases, the skull is broken into small pieces with heat. Their belief is with the help of the skull, by performing some ritual, they can control the soul of the deceased person, and this soul can be used as a ghost to harm others. This ghost can be sent to disable someone physically as long as this ghost is within the body. I have been through this myself.

Someone I knew, a family member in India, was not very happy with me. I was in my room in England, and one day I suddenly felt a jerk as if someone has entered in my body. My head area was normal, but instantly my body action was similar to being lazy, and it did not want to lift a finger to do anything. My body was disabled, even though I am a very energetic person. I gave it some thought for a day or two and pictured the involved person who wanted to harm me.

I did not hesitate to phone him, and I gave him a warning to go to the person he hired for this job. Otherwise, I will send the same treatment back to him and his practitioner. He did not admit to any wrong-doing, but I told him to go back to the practitioner and undo it or else. Within a few hours, I was back to normal. Now I knew who the culprit was. This can happen to any spiritual person, when one's spiritual armour is not fully on or there is some weakness in the aura.

If you know someone who is close to you and believes in this practice, do not cross the person's path and try to stay away. It does not matter how close a loved one he or she is. To you, these people are relations, but due to some reason, they consider you their enemy. Any practitioner, when reciting a psychic ritual, has attention that is single pointed, and he does not want or like any kind of interference, which acts as a divided focus and will not bring the expected results.

Practitioners summon the ghost, demon, or entity and command it to enter into the aura of the victim. These entities are fully controlled by the practitioner, but they can harm the practitioner as well, sometimes due to negligence on their part. These entities are no friend to anyone, and at times these entities can be very annoyed because they are trapped and unable to leave this world or communicate with loved ones to get help. One can imagine their frustration.

It is very easy for the people, who want to harm you, if they can manage to take something that belongs to your body: hair, nails, or any worn clothing (because the sweat of your body is still on the shirt). They all act as DNA to easily find your aura. Many use this practice in court cases to win over opponents. There are people who do not believe in black magic, but they believe in scientific evidence. It is individual choice what to believe.

I have seen many people fall on their backs by taking this practice very lightly. Black magic practitioners could act as white magic practitioners as well when a suffering person turns up at their doorsteps to get help. Practitioners can scan the problem and know what ritual to perform to undo the negative effect or spell. These practitioners are no friend to anyone; you pay them money to reverse the spell back to the sender. These practitioners are very lonely people, and no one wants to be friends with them because of their reputation.

They are not to be trusted. Only devious people hang around them, and they hold negative ideas. Some very skilled practitioners use clay pots (Kujji practice) to kill someone. They charge a large sum of money for this ritual. They prepare the small clay pot, probably a diameter of six to seven inches, and it is full of needles placed in a certain order. With the ritual, this clay pot begins to rise above the ground, fly and spin on very high speed in the air to the destined person (victim).

When it reaches the victim, it hit his or her body with full force, and all the needles get stuck in the body. This person is killed on the spot. During this ritual, the whereabouts of the victim must be fully known. If the victim is not there, this clay pot will return to the sender (practitioner), who is killed on the spot instead. Some families have property or financial claims. They are greedy and make sure all property must be theirs by hook or by crook.

This takes place between brothers, when one is innocent and the other is crafty. After the wedding, a newly arrived bride in the family trusts everyone and eats or drinks whatever is offered by family members. This greedy person will approach black magician to make barren the womb of this bride. Black magicians give something to mix in the food or drink as long and go in the body of this new member of the family. The lady will never have a child in her whole life.

These practitioners are charging very small amounts of money for this purpose, and someone's life is destroyed forever. How can one remove black magic spells? They can be removed from your body if you can hold lots of positive energy within yourself and leave no space for the entity to live. Sit in meditation and chant the word *Haiome* for a good twenty minutes. Visualise the white light entering your crown chakra and flowing within all over so that you are full of white light.

At the same time, visualise black energy leaving your body, and command it to not enter again. "In the name of God do not enter again." Quit by saying, "May the blessings be." Repeat this a few times to get the desired results. In my writings, you will find information on how to protect yourself from them, but sometimes followers do not read my spiritual writings thoroughly.

CONSCIOUSNESS

State of consciousness is a very common word amongst spiritual Seekers and religious groups. God means the total consciousness of the whole eternity, and we all are trying to experience part of it and feel blessed. Total consciousness includes all the spiritual planes, the total void, every single creature, and every particle or atom. Once, our great spiritual Master said creation does not exist in you or in me, but we have the power of creating to experience God's presence.

People often mention "my" or "your" state of consciousness, but I will say the success of any Seeker depends upon what you can create within yourself, with your own effort consciously. It determines up to which spiritual plane you can travel or within. That will be your state of consciousness; otherwise, it is all make-believe. According to our state of consciousness, we express ourselves to the outer world, and we are judged by people accordingly.

To live in the pure or highest state of consciousness, we must act in purity. God is the first cause; all others are second so that you can become Spirit. Satnam Ji is the greatest guru of all, appointed by God itself. He holds the second state of consciousness after God; the rest of the Masters or souls are third or fourth in line. Saint are those, who holds a high state of consciousness and yet striving further into the higher planes.

There is always a plus element, but we should achieve the highest state of consciousness we possibly can. In the olden days, it was very exciting to know that this saint was the sun god, especially in Egypt or India. At present we know the sun is only another planet and all planets orbit it. Similarly, there is worship of the moon in India and uncountable mythological stories. Now, we know it is only satellite to provide light on earth.

God is the macrocosm, and it expresses its presence through each microcosm. But to experience it on the physical plane is often distorted because of the mind and our emotions. The only way to know or understand is to dwell in this state of consciousness. This dwelling within is the art of separating soul consciousness from the physical mind's senses. As life unfolds with years, we must also unfold spiritually within or near to it every day.

Now, you do not depend on your religion to sort out your problems or ask for prosperity. You are in command to write your own destiny. People often ask, "Where is God?" Now you are in this position, where you cannot take your mind off God. You are always in communication with God. In this consciousness, repetition of spiritual sound, known as Anhad-Jap, is on the continuous within who wants to communicate with this world or mental thinking.

You have become one with Spirit. If you tell people what is taking place within, they may think that you are insane because it is beyond their knowing. In this consciousness, spiritual food, also known as God energy, is available. This way, you do not require any physical food apart from eating for formality to please others, such as when someone invites you for a cup of tea or food. The Master speaks with authority on divine wisdom because God has given him the spiritual mantle.

He is God-Realised and holds tremendous love for its creation. He is the true guru and light bearer for this physical world. This is why people often call him a true saint. Whoever holds this spiritual mantle or the torch bearer in the lower worlds means he is the only one person who can hold the highest state of consciousness for twenty-four hours. Although he holds this title, to him there is not an iota of excitement about it. Precious gems, gold, silver, or any number of coins do not attract.

He is always in peace within because he is always dwelling in spiritual fountain. These Masters are always appointed by God itself and the first personification of God, Satnam Ji, who is the ruler of souls and the soul plane. The present Master gathers as many souls as he possibly can so they can free themselves from the wheel of eighty-four. All the status people hold in this world—such as doctors, scientists, teachers, or thieves—are only different states of consciousness.

It is the result of guidance we received since childhood from our parents, society, or karma. This is the difference in lower or higher states of consciousness. We can reach or work towards God-Realisation, but maintaining that state of consciousness is a big responsibility. If we can maintain this state of living, then we can consider ourselves living the lives of saints. It is a continuous effort at the inner form via the means of spiritual exercises and contemplation on spiritual principles throughout the day.

Also, your outer form must express the inner spiritual fountain. In the beginning, we try to achieve a higher state of consciousness, and eventually it becomes a habit to dwell within a spiritual fountain. Many times, it takes a long time to realise this, or it comes to our attention that we have achieved what we were striving for. To know the whole truth, we must experience the supreme state of consciousness. This is only possible when you are so close to God, alone.

Now the question is, "Are we capable of doing that?" In this state of consciousness, you may be lonely but not alone. You are full of love, and the countenance on your face will express to the world. In this state of consciousness, you become the law unto yourself. The difference between this world and other spiritual planes is the state of consciousness. Those who are so close to alone often say, "My kingdom is not of this world," or, "I live in this world but am not part of it."

When you are the Master of your own universe, you will have little conscience towards any social virtues, values, or ethics of any religions in this world. All these social values are the basis of all priests to control the masses because you are free from social bondage that is very healthy for the soul and the key to physical longevity. Do not let yourself entangle with the social laws of any lower planes. In this way, you will not succeed on the higher planes.

This is why it is important to keep your state of consciousness within the spiritual worlds. It is your state of consciousness which makes you the Master of your universe and the captain of your destiny, if you can maintain it. It is your good karma which has led you to have a natural craving to enter into the worlds beyond your physical senses. Your spiritual success cannot be gained by imitating any successful spiritual traveller, but by right effort and action with every correct deed earned.

One day you will realise you are the image of God but clothed in rags and begging about everything in this world. Rightfully everything is yours to have, but because you have been brought up negatively, you have become the beggar. You have come to the realisation that it was only you, who has been holding you back from becoming the Master of your own universe. To achieve this state of consciousness; religious bases are to have good ethics and recite holy writing, which all the religions do.

To have any success, good ethics are needed, but they hardly play any part. It's the same with spiritual writings: they are only booster points, but to have any success, spiritual exercises and assistance of a spiritual traveller is a must. Ethics play a good part to cleanse the mind and prepare you to knock on the inner door. As the door opens, you experience the spiritual worlds, and the way they are cannot be explained in any religious scriptures.

The key to maintain your state of consciousness is your crown chakra. It is known by many names, and the soft spot or narrow is the way. As long as our soft spot is open, the Spirit can flow from above to within. This is only possible, when we are reciting our naam or word on regular basis. The more you can do this, the more Spirit will flow. A majority of the saints are able to maintain their states of consciousness due to this opening, whereas all priests are depending on book knowledge.

We often go to the saints to receive spiritual blessings. Being in the presence of a good saint and his state of consciousness also benefits us. It is always better to stay close to good people who have positive attitudes and lead highly ethical lives. We are representing God on earth as princes or princesses. We are the godly instruments (assistants) so that the Spirit can flow through us. It is this flow which maintains the balance in the lower worlds.

This is why we are known as the chosen people. It has become our responsibility to keep this spiritual flow as much as possible. That is only possible when we maintain our state of consciousness as high or pure as possible. If you are the chosen people, then it is guaranteed that you will never have to come back into the lower worlds. Without following the living Master of the time, you will never achieve this spiritual status.

Once you dwell in the higher spiritual worlds, you become the law unto yourself. We are able to make our own decisions, which are always based on our spiritual experiences, and that will supersede all laws which are man-made to mental satisfaction, also known as physical justification. Any action can be justified on the physical, known as punishment, but the individual still has to face the lord of karma.

All these wrong-doings and crimes committed are the result of physical or man-made laws. If people abide by spiritual laws, they will understand the responsibility of karmas being committed. Some religions do not believe in reincarnation or karma, so what can they teach to their followers? This is why they openly hold holy wars and yet claim to be religious. We all have five bodies, and all of them should be lived in a very balanced state.

Any person who is not in balance, especially in the emotional body, can lead us away from our real selves, our souls. The more our souls can express freely, the more or better our state of consciousness will be maintained. This is where most of the religious people fail: they always express the knowledge of their religious writings, but they never express their spiritual state of consciousness. I don't think they know the difference; it is beyond their knowing.

The subconscious mind is similar to our present-day computer system, where all our informative files are stored—even the ones we have forgotten. Only a few percent of our dreams can be remembered, but the memory of every single dream or any instance in life is stored naturally. This is the reason why some visions appear before us, and something reminds us, "Yes, I knew this before." How do you know that you are the holder of this higher God consciousness?

It is very similar to any fish because it cannot survive without water. You are always in communication with Spirit. People often ask, "Where is God?" I wonder sometimes and ask myself, "Is it true that they don't know where God is, and they cannot feel the presence of it? How can this be possible?" The majority of them are so religious, and if they cannot contact or feel God's presence, then I believe they must be knocking on the wrong door.

Physical or material sacrifices we make for Spirit is nothing, but in return what God gives you is an abundance of love, and there is no comparison. All those people who are proud of their religions or countries will never have, what I have written in this chapter. There is only one God, and all their religions and countries are walls between them and God. Remove these walls and walk into the arms of God. God is always waiting for your return as a spiritual assistant.

I am rephrasing an earlier statement, but religious people often talk about their state of consciousness. The question is, "What is your state of consciousness?" The soul has the power to create, as many believe, and the whole of creation is within us as well as outside us. Up to some extent it is true, but the whole creation does not exist in you or me.

A successful spiritual traveller is able to open up within, and then the whole creation of God and its spiritual planes can be visited internally or externally. How successful are you in opening up, and how far can you go? That will be your state of consciousness. If you cannot do either, you are no better than any person you know. This creative part will act as your yardstick to measure your success.

CREATION

Creation a vast subject and beyond us knowing, unless you are a spiritual traveller. There is a vast difference in spiritual knowingness and findings of science. Creation was created by the word of God—that is, Spirit and light and sound. The world of creation is finished for the lower worlds, and the original is within each soul to become spiritually aware of its existence and find its way back to its creator. We can have awareness of God's creation, but not fully of our creator.

As one saint said in the olden days, "The son wouldn't know the birth of his father." All religions try to express according to their knowledge, but I think it is all guesswork. I do not personally support the theory of evolution. To me, it is guesswork or a make-believe theory. Scientists are trying to guess the time factor by man-made equipment, which is a total waste of time. It astonishes me that all scholars of this world or well-known educated people, are in agreement that the whole of creation is original, but not humans.

For example, a cow is cow and a parrot is parrot, but we question our own originality. The majority of the world's population believes we progressed from a monkey species. We are also known to be superior and above the rest of God's creation. God created the system to run this system. God created nine "Super Souls" to look after all the universes. Then comes the living Master of the time to give message to all souls regarding what their purpose is in life and to help those souls who are ready to go back to their true homes.

That is the soul plane, and Satnam Ji is responsible for each soul. All the creation flowing out of God was carried through this first manifestation of God. Although all souls are created in Anami-Lok, each soul is a manifestation of God itself to experience. That is why it is a known factor that God is the creator and sufferer; he is the king and pauper at the same time. This is why God is the experience and experiencer at the same time.

The whole of creation is an expression of God, so whoever is addressing anything in the universes is God itself speaking, and it is speaking to itself. This puzzles the normal human mind as to, "How that can be? God created the higher planes, which are invisible, and their existence is in a beingness state, which is beyond matter, energy, space, and time. There is no action or reaction, day or night, light or shadow. Here is total brilliance, and these planes exist in a still position, which means they do not orbit.

Therefore, they are created as a flat surface. It was important to create Satnam Ji to represent itself as the first personification so that all created souls can communicate or see God in this way. Otherwise, no one can see God, although it can be communicated through divine light and sound. Under the supervision of Satnam Ji, lower worlds were created, and so were all the respective lords of each plane. Brahma, Vishnu, and Shiva are responsible for creating, preserving, and destroying all created physical bodies after learning of each soul's experience.

These three are responsible for both negative and positivity running in balance in the lower planes. The soul is pure in nature because it's a part of God itself. You may say it is naive in nature or an inexperienced soul. The soul is pure, but to experience or become aware of its true ability as part of God, it is given four lower bodies to create a puzzle or maze. In the beginning, all below the soul plane was a big void; only the Spirit existed.

It was totally peaceful, calm, and silent, with dim light appearing from the planes above. The mental, causal, and astral planes were created, and finally earth and the planets were created with light and sound in the shape of globe. It was called the Pinda world; *Pinda* means human body. Worlds of duality such as light and darkness only happened when these worlds became subject to matter, energy, space, and time. The Spirit began to plant the cosmic eggs of life forms.

The world was prepared with natural beauty first, water, greenery, fire, and oxygen to accommodate human life. Higher worlds are peaceful and blissful, yet there was spiritual immaturity in all souls, and so God decided to create lower worlds in the shape of learning schools for all souls. Satnam, Sohang, Ramkar, and Omkar Jot-niranjan are respective lords. Brahma, Vishnu, and Shiva act as Kal power to block the floodgates and make sure that each soul is fully experienced to be assistant in the worlds of being.

These lower worlds are known as physical, astral, causal, and mental planes. The lord of mental plane is responsible for creating the causal plane, and the lord of causal plane is responsible for creating the astral plane. The lord of astral plane is responsible for creating the earth or physical plane. Earth is controlled by the astral plane, and that is why all religions are talking about hell and heaven, king of the dead, ghosts and angels, and more.

All lower planes were created in a perfect manner spiritually and materially, light and sound, to nurture them forever. Nine Super Souls make sure that all of these planes run in balance. On earth, there are a number of other planets and millions of stars, and there is a space between each. This space actually has no existence; it is almost nothingness but is empty space filled with spiritual energy. We only experience the existence of space once an object moves from A to B or C.

It is the same with time, until and unless we measure or experience the events taking place. According to Hinduism's Vedas (religious books), in the beginning when the planet was capable of receiving the human life form, God sent its five princes. They were very close to God and were given the responsibility to guide the future souls arriving on earth. You may call them the first five saviours. The life span of these people was many thousands of years, and my spiritual finding or creation of God goes in line with Hinduism's Vedas.

We came into this world as humans and did not walk on four legs, as many believe. We are created in the image of Satnam Ji, and this is exactly what he looks like. Nowadays, science knows that it takes millions of years before any planet becomes capable of living. This physical planet is going to become barren land incapable of supporting human life in the next four hundred thousand years. Do you know that the next planet in line to accommodate new souls already exists?

I made a forecast in 2014 that it is going to be a new planet to receive new souls, but not as believed by most religions. At the end of this span, this physical plane will be empty for the same amount of four Yugas, known as Maha-Yuga. All the remaining souls will be put into deep sleep or will sit in a bliss state till Spirit makes this planet become liveable again. Nothing of the kind is going to happen. This planet will become abandoned land very similar to other planets, full of gases such as carbon monoxide.

At present, all scientists throughout this world are creating all kinds of nuclear weapons, and later those will fall into the wrong hands. People will destroy this world, and it will be incapable of supporting life like other planets. At present, Mr Kim Jong-un of North Korea and Mr Donald Trump of the United States are threatening each other with nuclear powers, and so does the majority of Islamic states. One day someone will be responsible for the world's destruction.

NASA and others are trying to find other planets for supporting life, but that's wasting time. In the past, all these planets were physical worlds at one time. There lived all forms of life very similar to this world, but due to their advancement in science, one day it led to destruction. At present, there are terrible gases, and no human life can be found, but it is possible to find some remains (skeletons). In June 2016, NASA managed to locate a new planet being formed which is three times the size of this planet. This will be the future physical world.

I wondered many times, when some religion said that God created this earth in six days and rested on Sunday. Today's science proves them wrong. Mind you, when the earth was created, the name of days was non-existent. Although God can create the universes within seconds, it did not happen that way. All our religions are the same, and there is too much mythology compared to reality. Mythology attracts the mind, which then wants to know, what the truth is.

Creation does not exist in you or in me, but God has designed this creation system in such a way that all souls have the ability to create a partial or whole universe. God is a big circle, and each soul has its own individual small circle. You are within the circle of God, at the same time God is also within your circle, and so is the whole creation. You are within the circle of every other soul too. There is a big circle, and all circles are within circles and within circles; that is the riddle.

The whole of creation is within yourself, and with some spiritual ability, you are capable of creating whatever you desire. The technique is to use your imagination in meditation and postulate to create, and then everything will appear on your screen. This is why all saints have expressed that God is within each soul, better known as the state of consciousness. You can see part of the experience of God once your soul awakens.

Many people ask, "Where is God? For example, the sun's ray upon the earth is proof of the existence of the sun." The sun's ray is not the sun but simply a projection of its substance. It is sustained by the sun itself. This existence of each soul on earth is a projection of the substance of God, and the soul is sustained by it. As another example, the whole tree is contained in the seed, and it requires time to transform itself into a visible shape.

In the same way, God and all its universes are sitting within each soul, but with experience we have to become aware of them. The amount of awareness we have will indicate whether we are Self- or God-Realised people. Light and sound are the means of its projection, and Spirit is food for the well-being of souls. At the end of a life span, the soul waits around in the astral plane till another child body is going to appear in the physical, but the karma of that family tree should match this soul to work out karma and further learnings.

By taking this new life, the soul is transferred to another field of action, and karmic account goes with it. No soul can detach itself from its accounts until they are settled. These accounts of previous lives are stored in the seed known as the causal body. Man or woman, when they become neutral, can be freed from lower worlds to enter into God worlds of being and become mini Gods, known as assistants. God created the sun and moon worlds at Sahasra-dal-Kanwal in the astral plane, which helps the souls to begin the inner journey.

During meditation, it is your creativity which helps to become aware of what already exists. The fact is that you cannot ever imagine something which already does not exist. Your imagination is capable of creating the whole of its creation. Man is related to the inner worlds through the subconscious mind, which stores most of the known and unknown information. All lower forms are limited in spiritual awareness, and they are still going through the process of the wheel of eighty-four.

Creation is finished and means nothing is to be ever created further; it is only manifested. The journey of each soul is a very long process, and it goes through eighty-four hundred thousand lives. The soul is immortal, begins its long journey, and enters into an elemental kingdom. From there, it passes into the mineral kingdom and then to rock imprisonment. Next it goes to vegetable and then the tree kingdom, which is a half-awakened state whereas the rock state was almost a full sleep state.

Next is animal, the bird kingdom, which is conscious and aware of its surroundings. After a long journey, the soul takes a human life form and begins to realise its individuality and awareness of its creator, God. Some of our lives are very passive, whereas others are very active. Passive lives are helpless because they cannot move from a given space or fight back, such as tree life. Animal life forms are fairly active, and they try to defend themselves by biting or running away.

Humans still want to hunt them for pleasure purposes, and that lands them on creating a high scale of karma. This becomes the cause of their suffering, amongst other misdeeds. Man, still denies any wrong-doing because it has the five passions of mind, which misleads in believing man rules others. When you rule, others act as slaves. There is another lowest creation of four elements. First are earth creatures, which are called gnomes; they are in charge of earth elements such as gold, silver, all metals, and minerals.

Next are salamanders, which are fire elements and look like small lizards or dragons. The next element is undines—for example, water spirits which takes care of sea life. The next element is the sylphs, relating to air spirits or fairies. After this long process, the soul enters human life and progresses to angels and total freedom from the lower worlds. To have any spiritual success, we must learn to love all of its creation; without love, there is nothing.

It is love that binds you to God, and it is also this love that unbinds you from evil and sets your feet on the path to righteousness. If you cannot learn to love all of its creation, you will never see the face of God or its representatives. Once you do see the face of the Lord, you will never be the same. In the higher worlds, here is true Spirit with no religion, nothing to travel, and nowhere to go—It Just Is. Lower worlds are known as a training ground for souls to learn to take responsibility of each action taken consciously.

Once you learn this truth, you are not far from your goal. The soul of each person is inborn and indestructible. It has no age, no classification in accordance to physical measures, and it is beyond matter, energy, space, and time. The soul is the experiencer and moulds into any given life form because of this ability. Two souls can occupy one body. When all other materialistic things need their own space to exist visibly, at the same time the soul is always an invisible entity.

After going through a long line of reincarnation system, you have attained lots of God awareness, and now you want to lead a spiritual life. Questions arise within: "Who am I? Where did I come from? Why I am here? Where am I going after death?" These questions will lead you to search for a spiritual guru, and one day you will be sitting in the presence of your creator. Once we have explored our learning in the lower worlds, it is time to leave this world and become assistants in heaven.

Successful people learn the art of spiritual travel and are capable of breaking the silver cord, not to enter into this world again. That is, leaving this world with its own freewill or you may go through some sickness to clear some remaining karma. The soul can leave through chosen spiritual chakra (it is normally the pineal gland), whereas others mostly use lower chakras. Leaving the body at the end is no more painful than birth. Accidental deaths can be painful.

Most animals face accidental deaths and are sometimes painful to watch. The soul is still within other wraps, known as mental, causal, and astral bodies, to face the king of dead. For those who have achieved spiritual freedom, their souls leave the physical bodies, and they remove astral, causal, and mental bodies on their respective planes. These bodies become obsolete with no further use, and they disperse naturally into nothing.

Dispersing the physical body becomes the responsibility of loved ones. Death indicates spiritual freedom and being in the presence of its creator, God, or returning back to life on the physical plane and clearing its remaining karma. I am not connected or a follower of any religion, and so I have written this on neutral ground because our God is neutral. There is only one God when religious followers are saying, "This is my God, and that is your God." This leads to their failure point.

May you know yourself and your creator, God.

DWELLERS IN GOD

Those who dwell in the presence of God are the most fortunate people. This is the ultimate goal of all spiritual Seekers, but only a few manage to make it this far. It is easily said but very hard to grasp, and it's even hard to maintain this state of consciousness. Only very few chosen souls can manage to do this. At the same time, in the background, Spirit or God is backing them up; otherwise it is very difficult in the lower worlds.

Every spiritual Seeker wants to dwell in the worlds of God, but only one person per million is successful. Many are making false statements. Following any saint for a few years or reading lots of spiritual literature does not make you a dweller in God. You have gained some mental knowledge, and you feel that you have become the knower of truth. When truth is many, many miles away from you, this is the difference between knowledge and knowingness.

You can only dwell in God when you breathe, smell, eat, hear, and sleep Spirit. In other words, when God has become your natural occupation of living, anything else is your second choice. These dwellers in God are true saints; although living in this physical world, their presence is always in pure in spiritual worlds and it always waits to follow God's instructions to assist wherever possible. They are true assistants of Spirit. They are the knowers of truth and lead others to do the same.

As far as this world is concerned, they become very lonely people, but they are never alone—God's presence is always with them. When you know that God is with you all the time, I don't think you want to socialise with anyone. There is nothing you want to know or discuss with anyone. Discussion with anyone in the lower world is a waste of time. What these people want to discuss with you is their problems. Most of their problems are self-created, and due to that, they are suffering.

Their problems do not interest you. Every suffering or problem is karma, which had to be paid for in full. Dwellers in God learned this long ago. They can guide others to not create any karma and pay back if any has been created. When any person is willing to sort out their wrong-doings and ask Spirit for guidance, it is always given. Dwellers in God are always silent, and they do not enjoy the company of others because people are often searching for human company to entertain themselves.

This whole world is meeting on a regular basis, and many cannot do without meeting friends every day. There are some who always want some particular person to not be out of sight all day; this is mental attachment. The majority of them are so busy making money or establishing their names in this world. All these things or ideas take your mind off God, and you can never be a dweller in God. Neither are those who claim to be so religious but are involved in some religious war, like a jihad.

These jihadists are misled, and those who do commit such acts are the victims of some altered destiny. There is so much anger sitting within, which is boiling inside to come out. Their anger is beyond control, but it is the wrong way of expressing it. You are going to kill someone whom you never knew or met. If the destiny of any person is changed by people around you, then the results are catastrophic. They could have been the dwellers of God, but there is something which keeps them away from it.

They are so close to God yet far, far away. When the saint becomes pure in his heart or in all his doings, and his dedication to Spirit has cleared all his karma, he can think of nothing but Spirit. Then reality appears. It is the purity that meets reality. Light and Sound overpower mental thoughts, and you lose interest in physical activities. You still are a physical person, but you do not feel part of it. With the feeling of music within and spiritual sensation all the time, you are dwelling within a spiritual fountain and are peaceful.

You cannot explain it to anyone, but people can see it on your countenance. Once you experience this, it is good enough to last for a lifetime. Those who dwell in Spirit all the time are fortunate and become assistants of God. Humans often want to leave their homes and meet others, or they are unable to sit in one place because they cannot still their minds. Very often they are searching for something to satisfy themselves. There is no patience and unbearable pressure in mind.

I hear from friends, and they say, "I just want to drop everything, pick up my bags, and go on seaside holidays." This is quite opposite to the dwellers in God; going on holidays, attending musical parties, and having any other celebration are very irritating to them. All these activities are a total waste of time, and they take your mind or self from the presence of God. To the dwellers in God, wherever they are, all their requirements are taken care of, although their needs are very small and basic.

They always dwell in the present moment, and no thoughts are given to the future. They do not pray or submit any petition for self; their faith in God is a law unto itself. Even if they don't get it, they are so content within with total satisfaction. The failure of most humankind is desire. They are never satisfied with whatever they have. Although the majority of people in this world are religious, religions are the basis of desires, and they are used as such.

The priest suggests one pray, and God will meet the desires. Priests wouldn't have a clue what God is or how to dwell in God. Humans often suffer because they live within a self-created world which is full of negativity. The dwellers live in God's worlds, which are pure and peaceful. In God's worlds, you simply be and enjoy; in self-created worlds, you suffer.

In search of peace, man knocks on many doors that are religions. There are many ways to go in, but once entered, it is very difficult to get out. This is the struggle most Seekers face, this is the point when a Seeker wants to move closer to God, but religion comes in the way. Religious scriptures often point "The Way to God", but followers fail to read and learn the correct contents of its direction.

May you find the way in and become a dweller in God.

———

FAITH

In our teachings, faith is total reliance in the Spirit and spiritual Master. This is the foundation of a spiritual journey into the inner worlds. Without faith, although you are following the teachings, you are more or less a sceptic. You must cross the boundary of doubt to become an open channel for the Spirit. Once you experience this flow, there is no turning back. You are the sailor who is exploring the ocean of God, where there is no beginning or ending.

Every thought or imagination turns into reality. Now you are the symbol of Spirit, and people look at you as the knower. Faith on this path is not same as religions. Their faith is based on a set of religious doctrine. They believe by following a set of religious doctrines, they will achieve their desired vision of God as dictated by their clergymen. All these followers believe everything is real, but it is nothing other than blind faith.

Do you know 99 percent of this world is living in blind faith to whatever is their concern? The setback of these people is that they do not have the guts to question their respective leaders. "What is your practical success in our religion?" Instead of giving a direct answer, you will hear a number of religious verses from their holy books, which are written by their religious founders. These leaders have left this world hundreds or thousands of years ago, and many holy books are written by their scholars (or at least updated by them).

This is the case of almost all religions. Ordinary people have a number of problems in their lives, and due to many fears, they respect their leaders and believe what they're told. Regarding these knowers of truth, if you ask them not to use your religion or the experience of your holy man, tell us what you know about God. "They will be dumb-stuck and lost for words because they never thought of God from that angle. This will act as a hammer on their heads and an awakening point in Spirit.

If they catch this point sincerely, they will never utter a single word to indicate this is "my" religion or that is "your" religion. All religious people have faith in their respective following, but unfortunately it is not leading them anywhere other than for or against other religions. Most of the wars are religious based. Each person carries a spiritual spark within, known as the soul. Ill thinking or killing another person is against the will of God, but these people who kill in the name of God feel proud and call themselves martyrs.

This is a clear indication that all religions are man-made to suit their needs or the circumstances. Any religious scripture written by a prophet leads the individual or soul to God, but later the clergy fails to convey a proper message to the followers, or they modify the true text according to their limited knowledge or to suit the demands of followers. Wrong interpretation of true text sometimes becomes a barrier between God and soul.

God created all the universes for souls to experience their personal spiritual journeys. These misled faiths have created a whirlpool where once you enter, there is no way out. Once in a while, some souls do find their way out; even then, they need guts to quit their following. Once you do manage to leave any religious teaching, the beliefs you followed for a number of years will still have a pull on you until your last breath in this world.

To be pure of religious thoughts, you need a very strong foundation and a spiritual teacher, who can create universal thought within yourself.

Universal thought is the beginning of any live experience. Once your journey begins into the inner worlds and you receive spiritual revelation or pearls of spiritual wisdom, your faith in Spirit will get stronger. Now you become the knower of truth. Now you don't need to follow any religious doctrine.

The answer to your questions will be at hand, and the more you tune in to Spirit, the more you will know. Your faith in Spirit is such that all your questions or problems will cease. Now you understand the system of God. God has created every person and situation for a purpose. All you have to do is to sail the oceans with ease. For any religious person, it does not matter how he prays. God hardly listens, but some problems resolve themselves with time or some other means.

The credit goes to one's religion or guru. Why does God not listen to them? Because their questions or problems are biased towards themselves. Hardly any religion is teaching the purpose of universal thought because they know once their followers have universal thought, the religions will lose their grip on them. Any person with universal thought is always a free entity, understands the meaning of free will, and will also allow others to be themselves.

Some religions are claiming to bring heaven on earth, and universal thought is the way. Though these religions claim to bring heaven to earth, in the backs of their minds, it is a well-established fact that "this is mine and that is yours". One day, Jehovah witness believers knocked on my door and persisted that I should read their monthly magazine because they wanted to bring peace on earth. As long as I was listening, they were very happy.

Once I told them that I had written a book about God, and I offered it very politely to them, they disappeared into thin air. You must practice what you preach. Their main purpose is to convert people to join them. All religions have very loyal members. The more loyal you are, the more religious you feel. Some religions ask their loyal members to donate 10 percent of their earnings. My question is, "To promote what?" The more you promote religious thought, the more ethical followers should be.

The majority of them are, but still it does not lead them to universal thought or individuality. God created each soul as an individual. Do you know even twins are not alike? You will find some difference in looks and in thoughts. Loyalty to any religion teaches the individual to lead a good, honest life, but it does not teach or guarantee one's place in heaven or indicate the time of one leaving this world. If the things don't appear or materialise according to your religious doctrine, your faith in the teachings will be broken.

Broken or shakeable faith can create catastrophic situations in your life, and you could be out of balance for life. The origin of new teachings or religion is always based on broken faith; the religion you followed was not as you expected. A majority of the religions spring out of another religion—for example, Sikhism out of Hinduism, and Christianity out of Judaism. Faith without any spiritual experience is not worth it; without proof, it holds no value.

Despite no experience, still there are millions of followers, and they will keep their faith alive because their ancestors said so. At present we are living in a civilised world with high standards of education. The majority of the religious thought or practice can be understood for its clarity. Blind faith leads you nowhere. God sends its messengers or prophets time after time to lead the souls back to God's worlds. They only serve the purpose to teach or show the way to be in the presence of God.

Once you learn this, there is no mediator between God and the soul. It is the individual journey of the soul. Once you have faith in Spirit or God and are unwaveringly loyal, I have no words to describe your spiritual gain. There are many fortunate people who do manage to find a true guru who has the ability of leading souls back to inner worlds.

During this union of Master and Seeker, many miracles take place. This will build up your faith more-strong.

But at the same time these miracles can divert you from your true seeking or original spiritual goal, you'd set for yourself. Faith alone is not good enough; the seeking within during meditation is very important. Once you become the knower of truth or reality, do you know this word *faith* also disappears now that you are part of Spirit? Your life will go along with the flow of Spirit. You will take any experience in life as the will of God.

Now you are so strong that no chains of this world can hold you to this physical ground. You fly like an eagle in the sky, and you will have the sight of a hawk who is watchful for all your karma, action, and reactions. Your success will lead others to have unshakeable faith, and one day they will be the sailors of the oceans of God and lead millions to do the same. Now you know it is the faith within Spirit and in your teacher, and nothing is impossible. There is nothing you cannot do or understand now that you know.

You are not here to pass time, but you are born to lead this world as well. During your spiritual journey, your faith will be tested many times by your teacher. Never feel discouraged. The Master is always standing next to you to make sure that you never fail. God did not create any soul, who is a failure. You are so dear to God because you are part of it. It will make sure that you return to God as a assistant. The more knowingness you have the more responsibility it will give you. One day you will return as a prophet of God.

A newborn child has natural faith in the arms of its mother, everything is provided without fail, and it has a smiling face. We struggle in life because we try to do things our way. Have faith in God, and you will receive all without fail.

—

FIRST CAUSE

The origin of everything is God. God is the first cause, and it created the spiritual planes and respective rulers. All the higher worlds are still part of this first cause. What it means is, there is nothing which is equal or opposite, plus or minus, day or night. These higher planes operate very much as God does, in pure Spirit. As we move below the dividing line or soul plane, that is where first cause turns into effect, and every action has a reaction.

This is when the battle of negative and positive begins. Whatever you see in this world is a reaction to or effect of this first cause, because God is the creator. In Christianity it is expressed through the story of Adam and Eve. They were placed naked by God in the Garden of Eden amongst all animals to live peacefully, and they were advised by God that they could eat any fruit from any tree except from the tree of knowledge.

This tree of knowledge was the key to crossing over the wall to see what lies on the other side. It is believed the serpent tempted Adam and Eve to eat this fruit. The serpent is a symbol of negative power. As soon as Adam and Eve ate this fruit, that acted as key to the awareness of negative power, and they began to think. Before, their minds were acting as spiritual minds. As soon as this happened, first they became aware of their nakedness, and all other negative powers or thoughts began to rise within.

They began to know who is human and who is animal. Self-protection is required from animal kingdom, it was not the animals who wanted to attack them, but it was the fear within and in their eyes. Animals only attack when they see the picture of fear in your eyes. Our belief in this theory of karma is different, we believe that the lord of karma attached some karma to each soul to begin its journey into the lower planes. By eating that fruit, Adam and Eve committed karma—or as Christians believe, the original sin.

All our sufferings are based on this original sin. Sexuality, fear, attachment, and all other passions came with this original sin. According to Christian texts, Adam and Eve were here 6,022 years ago, or around 4004 BC, when Hindu's written text is approximately ten thousand years old. I think Christian scholars need to make some corrections here. I only said things according to information provided on the Internet.

Negative power can blind any person to commit any kind of karma, and now we are so deeply involved in the world or the cycle of Kali-Yuga that we have totally forgotten about the first cause. That is why the question is often asked, "Where is God? Has anyone seen God?" Every person has created a fort around oneself. Anyone outside this **fort** is taken as an enemy. You will have very few near or dear ones, and any other is not accepted on many grounds such as religion, colour, and country.

God is the first cause, which is within each soul as a little spark. This is our link from soul to soul and from each soul to God. Due to too much negativity within yourself or around you, you may fail to see that person standing next to you is part of God and at the same time part of yourself. Then you have failed to see God. Why do you fail to recognise this spark in the person standing next to you? Because it is not your fault altogether.

At the same time, due to lots of negativity within that person as well, he also failed to express this spark within. You can see his actions and deceiving eyes, and you do not trust him. We have forgotten the first cause but have become the agents of Kal, and the veil of illusion covers everything. We always complain of our suffering. Why do we suffer? If we are suffering, then why are we complaining? Because we have forgotten our original sin or karma, which we committed, and now it is repayment time. When we fail to pay back, that is our negative quality.

The suffering begins through physical problems or physical ailments, and we cannot bear this pain. There is cause within cause and effect within effect. Every person or soul is a circle itself which covers the whole eternity. God is the original cause and the large circle, and we all are within God's circle. At the same time God is also within your small circle. This is the riddle that is so easy to understand, and at the same time it's complicated too.

—

FUTURE FORECASTS

This is a favourite subject of many people, but I have been avoiding for many years. I haven't written about it because once people come to know that you have said something, their curiosity compels them to find out more about it. I always tried to not get involved in this kind of discussion. Over the years, I saw so many visions of future happenings, but I lost the contents of them because I did not write them in my diary anywhere. Now I am going to write, very briefly, what I can recall, and I'll make notes on the future.

Helicopters

I mentioned this to so many friends or people in my circle, back in 1990. Approximately fifty years from now, the majority of cars travelling will turn into mini helicopters. As road traffic increases, future cars will fly in the air, and routes of travelling will be designed. Routes of travelling will be measured by different heights, and new drivers will pass their car tests accordingly. We can use uncountable travelling routes, and each vehicle will be limited or classed as to what route it can use. By 2040 or early, you will begin to see this in practice.

Future Destruction

I saw this vision back in 9 November 1994. A big destruction is going to take place in this world approximately thirty-five years from now, around 2030. It could be the year before or after, unless the vibrations of this world change. At present, all governments are very aggressive towards gaining power. I hope they can write some kind of mutual peaceful treaty.

New Earth Planet

The majority of religions are mentioning the end of the world. At present that is far, far away. As I said, a big destruction is going to take place around 2030. That will not be the end of this world but a big shake-up. After that, people will come to some positive realisation. The end of this world is approximately 400,000 years away from now. Once this happens, Spirit will shift remaining humans and other creations to a new planet. Not as mentioned by many religions that this earth will stay in darkness for the years of Maha-Yuga.

Then God will sprinkle Spirit, and this world will change into a new world, as it was originally. Maha-Yuga is the total combined years of four ages: golden, silver, bronze, and iron. I made this forecast back in 2012 to my friends that the new earth planet will be found soon, and that is going to be our future planet. I was very happy when I learnt that new planet has been discovered by NASA in 22 February 2017. It is three times the size of our present planet. There are a number of other planets yet to be discovered.

Weather Changes

Currently we use coal, gas, or electricity to warm our houses during cold weather. This is going to change. We have almost run out of coal, and soon we are going to run out of gas, petrol, and diesel. At the same time, we will try to not use them because of global warming. Nature has provided us with sunrays and water that, when used with new technology, will meet most of our needs. Windows of our houses will take complete transformation. They will provide and control the desired temperature within the house. At the same time, new glass will also act as curtains, moved with remote controls.

Future Housing

Skyscrapers have great architectural designs to be admired, however this is going to change. It is going to be hazardous living at these heights. Global warming and pollution of carbon monoxide will rise, and this will lead to many health problems. During the first and second world wars, underground nuclear shelters were made to protect ourselves. In the future, new houses will be built under the surface. This will be considered healthy living because it's scientifically proven that most of gases travel upwards. Heavy gases similar to LPG or any others will be discontinued. Underground living will be the pride of the future.

Population

The population of this world is increasing, however in the next five hundred years, it will show signs of decrease. In one thousand years, it is going to be the biggest worry for the whole world. People will begin to love each other and try to save whomever they can. At present, Kal is getting stronger by the day, but later on common sense will prevail.

Death

Death will be conquered in the future. Science is making very progressive strides in exploring other universes, and religions are failing followers in showing God's worlds, as mentioned in religious writings. Religions are failing to produce any true saints who can teach spiritual (soul) travel. Religions have become more or less materialistic and political. There will be independent saints who will teach spiritual travel, and our scientists will break the speed of light.

With this combined effort, people will be able to use both means to travel to other universes. At present everyone has a fear of death, but in the future people will be able to visit these places while still living.

Death will become the right of all people; either you want to live or die. Once this future travelling becomes a natural phenomenon, people will prefer to live in other worlds. Voluntary death and astral migration to upper regions will become tomorrow's world.

At present, most of the Third World countries want to migrate to Europe, Australia, or America. In the future, people will prefer to have relations on the astral plane or any other. As the chaos in this world increases, people will find there is no future living in this world.

Future Lie Detector

At present Narco test is carried out to find the truth behind serious crimes committed by suspects. This person being trialed is injected with Sodium Pentothal or Sodium Amytal or commonly known as "Truth Sermns". These drugs put the suspect into a semi-conscious state. So, during questioning, the required information can be obtained.

Second test is known as the Lie detector test, it is based on polygraphs. When questions are asked from the individual, it monitors the: Blood pressure – Pulse rate – Respiration and Skin conductivity to get results. These results are 95% accurate. However, this test has been known to be deceived by a very calm individual.

In the future both tests will be obsolete and replaced by new **vision test camera**. It will reveal the results as seen in the "Eyes". So, far we have over-looked the facts that there are two main culprits behind every crime or deceptions. It is your mind and two eyes. What you see, instantly is in your mind or vice versa. During questioning any suspect can tell lies but eyes are expressing, what is going on within your mind.

GOD-REALISATION

This is one of the simplest ways to explain what is Self-Realisation and God-Realisation, using these diagrams. For example, a drop of water (soul) is trapped inside this plastic dummy (physical body). It cannot get out unless someone can open it. This can only open if we have the Master to guide us, and with his help we manage to balance our five passions of the mind. Now we are aware of our lower bodies and understand their function during our journey into the lower worlds.

With the help of the Master, we have explored most of these lower spiritual planes. At present, we are on the verge of realising ourselves as souls. Once we find this opening and manage to travel internally or externally on our own, we can know our true identity is soul, not the physical body, as we understood for years. This is the first step of realisation. There is a lot more to know and understand. At this point, we should live our lives as directed by God or Spirit.

Drop of water as Soul

Soul trapped inside body

Now we have found the opening
Soul is free to explore.

Glass of water as symbol of God
Ocean of love and Mercy.
Now becomes part of Ocean.

Now it depends on your effort and for how long or up to what extent you can live your life as directed by God. That will lead you to have God-Realisation in this life. Once you are in a God-Realised state, it depends on how long you can dwell in this state of consciousness. It is a big responsibility to maintain this state of consciousness; otherwise you could be Self-Realised only. The higher you go, the easier it is to drop from your position.

May success be yours.

GOD'S EMPIRE

All religions are claiming their empire or the number of member-ship they have, how dominating they are, or what their growth will be throughout this world. They have very clever ideas to spread their message. Some religions are losing membership because they have failed to accommodate the expectations of their followers. The whole of creation, known as souls, are part of God. Due to this spiritual link, they cannot be separated from God.

The total number is very similar to our bank accounts. For example, I have five different bank accounts, and I have placed different amounts of money according to my needs. My one account holds £6000, another has £5000, and the rest three are holding total of £1000. The total is £12000. As long as my original total remains safe and sound, it should not bother me mentally which account holds more or less.

It is same with God. As long as all souls are learning their experiences in the lower worlds, it does not bother God because all the lessons cannot be learned in one religion or in one system. All those religions claiming large membership are pride for their religious leaders, but to God, its children are playing with toys. Which child has more toys than another? Does it matter to God? No, because at the end of the day upon counting, God knows that they are all his.

This is the point all religions fail to understand. They are fighting with each other while not understanding who is the boss and owns every soul. To any religious body, they are their followers. One day they will know and understand. In this discourse, I will try to explain very briefly the whole structure of God. There is an infinite void beyond human measurements, and this void is full of silence. In the centre is God.

God is formless and beyond any known limits. God does not take any form because it is part of the whole creation. Its creation has 8,400,000 facets, and on this basis, it is part of every single face. At the same time, it has none because it is within each soul, and so no one can claim God looks like him or her. God has kept itself in a neutral basis. Similarly, we can see or experience our mirrored image of God once we reach any understanding of it, known as spiritual unfoldment.

God is known by many names in many religions. The names are used according to their experience or how close they have managed to be in God's presence. God, Allah, Hari, and Prabhu are the names given or suggested by the founders of each religion, and their followers believe these are the true names of God. To God, it does not matter how you contact it. Learning of spiritual experience in the lower worlds is important and known as schooling for soul.

Light and Sound

Communication of God to its creation throughout all the planes, universes, and planets is based on twin pillars, divine light and sound. Light is knowledge and provides illumination and existence of all creation; otherwise, all creations would have been there, but visibility to each other would have been none. Sound is the bonding part to put all the particles together and in different arrangements. Combination of both is known as Spirit, which sustains the entire creation.

Awakened souls can feel the presence of Spirit, and more awakened ones can feel the presence of God too. Awakened souls can also see the light in many shades and can hear the sound in many melodies. Light is a pure, brilliant white shade, but as it travels from God through the higher planes and then proceeds into the lower planes, its shade or colour changes according to the vibrations: pure white, light golden, golden, purple, blue, orange, pink, and green.

Sound also changes its melody as it passes from higher to lower worlds: silence, whirlpool, woodwinds, a thousand violins, a humming sound, wind, flute, buzzing bees, running water, tinkling brass bells, the roar of the sea, and thunder. Light and sound as Spirit are invested in each soul to keep this communication alive so that all souls can feel the presence of God. It also knows the well-being of each soul.

Sound is also known as Anhad-Shabd or Dhun-Atmic, which is also on continuous rolling within each soul; this is known as the lifeline of each soul. Sound flows from God's worlds to the lower worlds and travels back to its original source. This flow is known as centre petal and fugal. These are the sound waves for each soul to travel back and forward to its creator. Sound acts as a vehicle, and light acts as knowledge or a torch to see the spiritual path. The number of these waves is infinite to accommodate the whole creation.

Nine Pillars of God

I don't think religions are aware of what I am going to say, apart from one or two paths. I call them the "Nine Super Souls". They were especially created by God to assist in creating all higher planes and keep maintenance of all spiritual planes, universes, and Planets. Super souls are only answerable to God itself and repair any unbalance created by negative vibrations.

If these Masters are not here, it will not take long to explode stars, the heat of the sun will be unbearable, and the outcome will be disastrous. Many of the disasters are due to this unbalance or are created by the nature to maintain its balance. Nine Super Souls do not communicate with any person or being, and they move along silently to do their spiritual endeavour as required or advised by God. To investigate situations, they may take the form of a tree, mountain, or anything else.

God's Worlds

God's worlds are created to accommodate many other required facilities. Anami-Lok and its lord, Anami-Purukh, are responsible to create new souls. At the same time, this is the only plane where souls are purified for a special purpose. Although all souls are pure as part of God, when the new living Master of the time is given the responsibility, then his soul is taken back to its original creation point to do clean-up of any impurities. Due to this clean-up or creation of souls in this plane, that is why it is called the plane of love and mercy.

As for Agam-Lok, if any soul manages to come this far due to its spiritual unfoldment, the soul becomes aware of its creator, known as God-Realisation. The soul knows, "I am not only a soul but am part of God." Very few saints have managed to come this far. Golden temples in the Alakh, Alaya, and Hakikat planes provide spiritual education for the soul so it can have God-Realisation. All these planes have their respective lords, and their titles are material based. I cannot think of any suitable words to express their beingness.

Satnam Ji

Any of the above lords are not to be seen by any soul to communicate. When required, they purposely manifest for the experience of any soul when taken by the Master of the time; otherwise, these beings remain invisible. After the creation of all, any soul is housed in the soul plane. Souls on this plane are visible to each other for relevant communication. Although God is neutral and formless, this is the requirement to create a link between souls and God. God manifested itself as its first personification, known as Satnam Ji.

This is why in Sikhism it is known as Akal-Murat. Akal is opposite to Kal or negative power, and therefore Akal means formless and Murat means replica. Satnam Ji is the replica of God for any soul to be seen or communicate with. Upon this meeting of soul and Satnam Ji, the silent voice within feels, "I am He, and He is me." Materialistically speaking, the soul plane is the storehouse for all souls. Satnam Ji becomes the keeper of all souls and keeps the record of each soul's journey from the beginning till it becomes God-Realised.

This is why Guru Nanak of Sikhism called Satnam Ji Karta-Purakh, which means responsible for all souls. God gave Satnam Ji the responsibility for all souls and for being seen when this communication is required. A soul, as the replica of God, is neutral in nature and has its being in the pure spiritual planes. There was not much learning for souls. Anami is the creator, and Satnam Ji is the caretaker of souls.

Vairaagy Masters

These Masters play very key role in God's empire. "You may wonder who are they? In God's empire, there is no such time when God does not have one representing its message. This is a chain or unbroken line of Masters, with all those Masters who have done their duties in the lower worlds and are gone beyond, but a few selective ones remain behind to assist God, present living Master, Nine Super Souls, or the lord of planes.

God

God created the lower planes and trinity lords to look after its new creation. It is pure Spirit in higher worlds but divided into negative and positive in the lower worlds. All the lower worlds are based on this duality. At any time, no one can claim, "I am as pure as God," while residing in the worlds of Kal. Kal is name given to this spiritual power to provide schooling for each soul.

Multiple tasks were created by Kal power for souls to pass through so that it can learn lessons to become assistants of God. New embodiments are given to each soul as garments to wear, according to the number of planes, so a soul can express itself on each plane. Mental, causal, astral, and physical are planes, and each soul is covered by these layers or bodies. Each layer will be eliminated with our spiritual experience until it sheds all layers to become a pure or neutral soul, itself in pure Spirit.

This is why we use the word *unfoldment*. The soul was folded within these layers to be unfolded. Lower worlds are vast in size, and there are a number of lords or keepers, but a new trinity was created to take care of souls' welfare in the lower worlds. All religions have different names, but in Hinduism they are known as Brahma, Vishnu, and Shiva.

Trinity Gods

Brahma is the creator of lower bodies. Vishnu is known as the preserver, and his responsibility is to provide food or shelter. Shiva Ji is known as the destroyer, and so every lower body has to be destroyed after its allotted time. In the lower worlds, nothing is permanent. Whatever body—man, animal, tree—is given limited time before it ends one spiritual experience and begins a new life. This system is called the wheel of eighty-four, and each soul has to incarnate time after time for a number of lives to mature and become a assistant of God.

Shakti

Female energy is worshipped around the world by many different names. It is considered as the mother of this world. In Hinduism, it centres around the incarnation of feminine power, known as Kali Mata. She is worshipped similar to Brahma, Vishnu, and Shiva. The importance of Mother Goddess is that Brahma creates, but for birthing a child, one needs a womb. Vishnu is the preserver, but the child needs someone to feed him. This is why and how the female energy helps in the creation of God's empire.

Maze

A maze was created by these lords for our schooling to help us learn and get purified. A number of attachments are given (five passions of the mind), and so we are busy with these passions: Kam, Krodh, Lobh, Moha, and Ahankar (lust, anger, greed, attachment, and vanity). This is the puzzle, and the soul had to find a way out to become free once more. So negative or Kal provide the chain and spiritual Master is here to free the soul or show the way of getting free.

Karma

As soon as any soul leaves the soul plane and goes into the lower worlds for schooling, karma is attached to it to monitor the soul's progress. As we socialise in the lower worlds with other souls, now the soul is covered by other four bodies: mental, causal, astral, and physical. On the physical plane, the physical bodies are representing souls to each other.

Lower worlds are an illusion and impermanent, but illusion and the five passions are so strong that a majority of the population has forgotten there are souls. They believe that minds and physical bodies are the main players in the lower worlds for survival. This is the reason people suffer.

Suffering

Suffering means going through some experience, either positive or negative. Suffering means the soul has learnt some lesson or become aware of some spiritual point, known as unfoldment. The soul is the knower of truth, being part of God itself, but it must explore every single point or situation. The five passions are there to incarnate desires within, and each desire will lead the soul to learn another lesson. Kal-Niranjan, or negative power, creates situations for the soul to pass through every lesson with distinction.

But a majority of the religions are teaching that negative power is bad. This is the statement given by very weak people or religions. Every single lesson is a step forward and towards the Creator. We live our lives emotionally based, with attachment to our relations. Our weaknesses push us towards God for any mercy. Why are we looking for this mercy from God or any saint? Because we cannot bear the pain of our suffering or what we have created.

During our incarnations and dealing with other souls, we overlooked or did not pay back what we borrowed from others; it could be food, money, property, or physical care. What is suffering is the karma we are going through, where someone else is in the commanding position and we are weak or with less authority. This suffering could be in the shape of mental or physical torture, but we have forgotten that we did put this person in a similar situation too.

In the lower worlds, no one is doing any favour to anyone, or we are not suffering without any reason. It is the theory of action and reaction, equal and opposite, cause and effect, and yin and yang. We are always happy and enjoy receiving gifts, but often we feel irritated when repayments are demanded. It is only exchanging of karma, and it is always recommended to create good karma, which means learning to give instead of receive.

Spiritual Master

Negative power creates the situations according to our karma. The spiritual Master shows us the way to go through the situations with ease. The spiritual Master is the key player in God's empire, He is everywhere, from the God to the physical plane, and all souls from any plane can contact him for assistance. His authority is consented by God. He is not head of any religion or chosen by the public, whether religious or politically based.

His birth is planned by Satnam Ji and the lord of karma to prepare ground for his birth, from where he will be able to give the message of God. He is from the unbroken line of Masters since the Golden-Age, and he will continue till end of Kali-Yuga (Iron-Age). This line of Masters will not remain for too long in one country. It'll be no more than one or two Masters, and then it must shift its spiritual centre to another country, where the presence of this Master is needed.

His only purpose in life is to lead souls back to Satnam Ji. That is why he is not a reformer, as most of the saviours claim. Reformers bring change in some part of this world. God has created the system for the benefit of souls' learning. If this seat of spiritual power remains in one country for too long, then it will not take long for pure, individual teachings to turn into new religion. Reformers deceive this purpose. God can bring change to any system in a split second.

Religious followers or leaders are happy with reformers because they try to make life easier, and all is temporary. Reformers are sympathetic with humans, and it is the quality of Kal or lower worlds. God operates beyond duality on a neutral basis. The Hindu saviour Krishna came and brought the change. Napoleon, Alexander the Great, and lately Hitler have tried to bring change according to their ways of thinking.

Any change which is not in line with the planning of the lord of karma upsets the system and alters the purpose or destiny of souls. All these killings done in the name of religion or politics serve no purpose other than to delay the soul's journey. Holy wars were fought in all religions over thousands of years. We are still the same people, moaning, groaning, and fighting. As long as we are in the lower worlds, this will carry on forever. Reforming the system is temporary solution.

God does not give authority to any person, religious leader, saviour, or reformer to take the life of another human or any of its creation. Truth often hurts. Any saviour who holds a weapon to kill another creature or tries to show authority in this manner is in violation of spiritual law. God does not kill or destroy any soul whatsoever. Then who are we to do this? All these religious saviours are our heroes, but they are very small players in this empire of God.

We should try to lead any person who we believe is of wrong-doing to do good karma. Ending his life does not serve this purpose. In his next life, he might do worse. Any person who wants to leave this world must become universal in thought. He may be born in any religion, but he must accept all creation as part of himself. Be yourself and let the others be. If you cannot do this, then you have created a wall between yourself and God, and you will never be a key player in God's empire.

The teachings of these living Masters are beyond religion and will remain that way. He is not the heritage of any religion or country. He is normally shy in nature and not known by many. By the time people find about him, he is already gone from that arena.

Lord of Karma

Karma is attached to every soul upon leaving the soul plane, and spiritual progress of each soul is based on this. Every incarnation will teach the soul from a different dimension, and there are millions of tasks we have to go through. The lord of karma places the soul at certain places through birth, which give the soul the best opportunity for learning.

We often take this learning point as suffering. At the end of the soul's present physical life span, the lord of karma sends the angels to bring back the soul in its presence and records the learning in the register. Depending on what you have not learned yet, he will place you somewhere on the physical plane for your next task.

Heaven and Hell

There are sections in his place where each soul is kept till, he prepares a suitable place for next lesson. Religions often call this place heaven and hell. Many dramatic or scary stories are told by priests to scare people. They tell these stories because I can guarantee you, they have never seen the places themselves. Each soul is very precious to God, being part of itself, and each soul is sent into the lower worlds to gain spiritual experience so that it can become assistant of God.

We send our children to school for learning, and they do many wrong-things. Do we hang them upside down to punish them, or boil them in hot water or oil? No. We try to show them the way so that same mistake is not repeated. The lord of karma does the same. Instead of punishing, he sends us down again in this world till we execute that learning and pass with distinction. The lord of karma and all situations are created for our learning; this is why all these lower worlds are known as illusion.

This is God's empire to create souls and bring them into the lower worlds. The lords in each plane help the soul to learn further. In some future discourse, we will discuss many spiritual bases to control and keep balance of all universes. They are the way stations to communicate with higher planes for the landing of UFOs. Spiritual scriptures provide knowledge for souls who are ready to work with the spiritual Master of the time. He will lead each soul through a journey to golden temples, and eventually he'll lead the soul to its true home, which is the soul plane and above.

Non-believers

In the modern scientific world, you will find non-believers of God. Why they don't believe? They have many reasons because some how they do not feel the presence of God in this world. It is not God who failed them; it is their birth religion which failed to express the presence of God. They always talk about their guru, who was sent by God to convey its message. This guru was here for few years, but now he is gone, and it becomes a dead religion because the flow of Spirit is not there as it used to be.

Followers still believe the Master is still around, but the new caretakers (priests) don't know what to do. They create a system, where it is less of religion and more of politics. Some sincere Seekers do not feel the presence of God as they believed to be in their religion, and they lose faith and walk away from it, saying, "I don't believe God exists." Many times, you will notice these non-believers or sceptic people become the true followers of God. They are waiting for a spiritual spark to be seen from somewhere, and then they are live again.

The living Master is here if anyone wants to experience God or its empire in this life. There are so many yoga systems that practice the Kundalini. If anyone wants to experience psychic powers known as illusion, then you can follow this route. God has provided the answer to every question. It is up to you to know or ignore the answers. That is your free will. But never say God does not exist.

GOING BEYOND PHYSICAL

All the lower worlds are subject to duality and so they have a number of suns according to the light required because they are more luminous than the physical universe. All higher planes have flat surfaces. The reason for this is that they are beyond time or any duality, and so they do not have to orbit to acquire any illumination. Souls do not sleep because as part of God, they are always in the arms of Spirit.

This is a small riddle which most of the religious people don't grasp. Most of the religions will never know what higher planes are because they are all stuck in the heaven and hell area. Their discussion always revolves around these two words. This universe is so vast that to travel physically takes long time. Can you imagine if you have to travel all the lower worlds and the worlds beyond? How long will it take? This is one way of travelling, but our creator has made our journey so simple.

It's very similar to our present computer science. God made attachments or folders full of details of all universes or planes ever created. All you have to do is to open these files, and the totality is shining or opened up within yourself—and exactly on the spot where you are sitting. The key to open these files is your soul. On the same basis, there is no space in pure spiritual planes, and nothing exists because each soul exists within each other.

This is why there is no time or space to travel: you make up the point to be present at, and the soul will shift or find itself present here. This total space or void is occupied by God itself, and you are part of it, so consciously you are everywhere. Upon leaving, you will find the astral plane is better than our physical plane and its laws, as it is supposed to be because of the presence of Dharam-Raj or the king of the dead. The court of this judge is always open because there is no such time when souls do not leave the physical plane.

There is no waiting time for anyone; your earned deeds have to be justified there and then. How you can pay off your outstanding karma is decided between the king of court and the soul. A heavy karmic pattern often drags the soul back to the physical. Although there are two sections known as heaven and hell, you are placed according to your remaining karma. It is similar to our railway tickets when travelling first or second class. There are no horrible places as mentioned by the priests to create fear within its followers.

Heaven means your karmic pattern is not that heavy, and so you may remain in this part of the astral plane to work out remaining karma and progress to the next heaven, known as the causal plane. Hell means you remain there till a place of birth is prepared for you. God sent souls into the lower worlds for schooling so they can assist in its cause later. A description of hell clearly shows the depth in knowledge of any religion. The soul is not a waste; it is part of God itself.

Therefore, it is very dear to God, and it is cared for while waiting for next incarnation. If you are travelling with the spiritual Master, that is very healthy. Otherwise on the astral plane, there are good souls who assist and lead you to your earned place or group of known people, such as relatives. The soul represents in the astral form, and similarly the soul represents itself on the physical plane in a physical body.

Religions or priests are always talking about the heaven and hell on the astral plane concerning people leaving the physical because this is all they know or have heard about in their religious scriptures. This is all book knowledge, "What happens to those souls who are progressing from astral to causal or from causal to mental? Similarly, each plane has its own lord of karma and decides the fate of each soul. When a soul reaches the soul plane, it is beyond the karma zone, and it comes directly under the supervision of Satnam Ji.

Now the soul is karma-less, and so it does not have to return into the lower worlds because it has attained spiritual freedom. Achieving spiritual freedom is very simple, or it could be very difficult depending on how you approach this experience. Your spiritual Master will guide you to follow some instructions. The base of your success depends on how successful you are in doing your spiritual exercises. Very briefly, prepare yourself for spiritual exercise. Sit down in tailor fashion in a quiet room.

Keep your back erect and your chin slightly up so your crown chakra, the third eye, and spine are in line. This helps Spirit to enter through the crown chakra easily and reach all other spiritual points. That stirs the vibrations when reciting your spiritual word. Imagination will play a great part in achieving your goal. As your vibrations are stirred up, we have a very warm feeling within our foreheads, and our bodies feel a slight vibrating sensation. If we can hold on to our nerve, the soul will leave through the tenth door in no time.

You will find yourself in the sub-planes of the astral plane. In turn, you will see the sun world zone, and then comes the moon world, and then lighting world zone (Ashta-Dal-Kanwal). This is the place where your spiritual guide is waiting for you. The Master will meet you in his radiant form, and that will change the course of your future life because you are not the same person. You can consider yourself spiritual traveller as well. Sahasra-Dal-Kanwal is the capital of the astral plane.

GOLDEN AURA & BLACK MAGIC

Those who are following the living Master with full sincerity are fully protected by the spiritual force. As you recite your spiritual word, and it is on continued recitation at the inner, then Spirit provides a spiritual shield. Wherever you go, you are within this shield. It does not matter how hard someone tries to harm you—it will not work. You will find lots of people around you who are not happy due to many reasons. They live under the influence of anger, one of the five passions of the mind.

Sometimes this anger alone does not satisfy them, and so they go a number of steps forward and seek psychic help. This is to make sure that you are truly hurt in some way. This is a very pleasing experience for them. A majority of time, you will find they are claiming to be very religious people, but they do not apply any spiritual principles in life. Anger has crowded their mentality. Now, what happens when they send anger or black magic towards this true spiritual Seeker?

The Seeker is always within this invisible golden or white light. Anything sent towards him bounces back to the sender. Once this burst of anger energy or black magic cannot penetrate the spiritual shield, it generally returns to the sender, who is injured by his own act. This spiritual shield is a law unto itself, and it has the power to return whatever is coming towards it to the sender. This holy person is not responsible for whatever happens to the sender.

In this situation, the holy person is not a cause or effect. This sender or angry person is the cause of this situation and the effect of his own doing. You shall reap what you sow, as the saying goes. If you are following the teaching of the present Master, then Spirit acts like a mother hen who spreads her wings over her chicks to cover them when an eagle or hawk hovers over them. Little chicks have full faith in the mother hen for protection, and we should trust the inner Spirit.

Once we are tuned in Spirit, we are living peaceful and happy lives. Did you ever see the baby struggle in its mother arms? The answer is no. We only suffer or struggle in life when we are scared and move away from the wings provided by the Spirit.

Trust Spirit, because nothing can touch you.

GOLDEN HOUR

The golden hour does not happen often in our lives. It is very rare moment, and we often miss the opportunity to enjoy it, thinking there is plenty of time. It is the moment when you could be sitting in a blissful state. I know the time, when you were sitting in a blissful state, and this is the time, when most people are afraid. I am talking about that time which is before your birth in this world. This scary place is called heaven or hell in our terminology.

This is the time when you previously had completed your physical journey, and through the experience of death, you end up in the house of the lord of karma. You have been judged according to your deeds, and now you are waiting for the next suitable family appointment. You'll find a suitable family according to your karma, or your karma should match within some good family, but there is no opportunity for any birth taking place because there is no married couple at present in that family who could bear a child.

It may take a number of years before anyone could get married in that family to welcome your arrival. In this situation, you are waiting in the home provided by the lord of karma. It is care-free period, and you have been cared well by the lord of karma. I call this your golden hour. The next stage of the golden hour takes place at your birth. The child is always welcome in our civilised society. You bring joy to the parents and family.

The love you receive is in abundance: cuddles and kisses all day, you are well fed and bathed, and your smile brings joy to all around you. It is a golden hour to your parents because their wish has been fulfilled. You have nothing else to do apart from eat, sleep, and smile. You are so happy. Do you know why? Because you don't even have the knowledge of your birth. Sometimes you may not feel well or have some pain. You do acknowledge pain but have no fear as elders do.

Do you know that during these early days, months, or years, you do not even acknowledge if you die because you don't even know what death is? You only acknowledge the death once you become aware of yourself in this world. In the early days or years, you enjoy playing with toys. As long as you are playing with toys, that means you still have not established yourself in this world. During early death, your parents will cry because you left a very deep scar in their lives.

It is the amount of love you have given them and your company that they enjoyed. To them it is sorrow, but to you it has been a golden hour because you never knew what is death or fear. This awareness of birth may take three to four years, or it may take up to seven years. Once you are aware that you are part of this world and know what is pain, then your experience of life becomes painful. You feel your pain and others' too, and then your golden hour is fading away as responsibilities of life increase.

As you enter the teen years, it could be painful if your parents have separated or your background is poor. But to some, the golden hour continues through these years. Your family needs, education, or playing sports are all placed in a golden hour for you to enjoy. At present, the golden hour is depending on your background. At this age, you are fully aware of yourself. Man's suffering, is the result of his own doing; we often become careless to our surroundings.

The more you love God's creation, the more God will give you abundance of love. If you don't care about its creation and become violent, then it is not God who does not care about you, but it is your own doings you have to face. With time, your golden hour seems to fade away, and you are surrounded by lots of sorrows. Now you are married, and your responsibilities increase, including providing for your children. They could be ok, or it is beyond your control to commit such acts.

With time, your golden hour fades away like an old dream which once you dreamed, and now it only appears as a shadow in your memory. Now it is time to experience the hour of love—that is, if you are fortunate enough. Or it could be hour of total darkness. It is a big void, and the golden hour seems far, far away similar to fairy-tale stories. At old age, physical pain increases, and the people you loved may disappear. This is the experience of life, which you never knew before, yet many more situations are to come and teach the truth of life.

Life has taught you how to love, and now it is time to learn detachment. You have to learn the art of living, and once you become the master of life, it is time to leave. Your loved ones can see that you are almost ready to die. They cry and pray for your safe journey. They hold your hand, and you feel nothing, or you can hardly hear what they say. It is your last hour, and you are looking at them. They are looking at you and wondering why, because you are there but are dwelling in different place.

As the body becomes numb, you feel no pain. You are waiting for the moment to leave. Angels have arrived, and you are pointing the finger at them. They smile to accompany you. You can hear the lord of karma doing your accounts; if any disturbances or cries interfere, you tell everyone to be silent. That moment of crossing is most important to you. You point at any closed door to your loved ones to open with a cute smile on your face. Your last breath has stopped.

People around you begin to cry, but your golden hour has just begun. You follow the same landscapes of the astral plane—the greenery, flowers, hills, and paths you walked not long ago. They all seemed familiar because you were there only a few days ago, although it had been many physical years. You feel fresh because some kind of burden has been taken off. You are back in the blissful state, and the lord of karma is taking care of you until your next assignment.

There are millions of people sitting in the golden hour when billions of you are afraid of going there. It is your golden hour. For how long? That is the will of God. I have learned a lot, and there is a lot more to come. Until then, let me enjoy my golden hour. You can enjoy this blissful state or golden hour if you can learn the art of dying daily, known as spiritual travel within. I have learned this long ago, and it is the most peaceful moment, continuous is-ness, which is never ending—unless someone comes and throws a little stone.

Then you see the disturbance in still water, and small waves form. In physical terms, it is called the company of others. To this world it is company or friendship, but to the saints it is disturbance. This is why they prefer to stay alone but are never lonely, because as the creators of the whole universes, someone is always with them. One day you may learn to be alone and enjoy this golden hour here and now. I know God and it also knows me. To me, nothing else matters.

This golden hour may be yours.

———

GOLDEN TEMPLES
& GUARDIANS

Guru Ji

Guru Ji was the first Master to represent God on earth during the Golden-Age. Ever since, this line of spiritual Masters is continuous through today and will do so until the end of this physical world. First, God sent five humans to earth, also known as the five Princes, and Guru Ji was one of them. The reference to the first five humans (Panch Raj-Kumara's) is also mentioned in original Hindu (4 Puranas) religious texts that are part of the Vedas. This is also my personal experience.

Rebazar Ji

Before, we go into the temples and guardians, we must mention our greatest and youngest spiritual Master, who still maintains his physical body and was born in the mountain village of Sarranh during 1461. That makes him 557 years old this year. He is from Tibet. He is approximately five feet ten inches tall, has black eyes, and weighs around ninety-five kilogrammes. His short hair and black beard are cropped closely, and he has very distinctive mark in the middle of his bottom lip. He is approximately eight years older than Guru Nanak, who was born on 14 November 1469.

His mission is that of a messenger for "The Way to God", spreading the word throughout this world. He normally reaches the Seekers by direct projection. His residence is in the western Himalayan Mountains near Tirich-Mir, one of the highest peaks in the world. He wears a knee-length dark maroon robe, always holds a wooden staff in his hand, and wears wooden sandals (kharava) on his feet. He has small mud hut to live in for physical use, and there are more saints with of similar age or older living nearby.

Other Spiritual Cities

There are nine Dhamas or pilgrimage spiritual cities for the Seekers to visit and learn the wisdom of God. The way to reach these spiritual cities is via spiritual travel accompanied by a living Master of the time. Locations are marked in the God world chart. The purpose of these cities is to provide bases for the magical forces of this planet for smooth running, as well as way stations to reach other spiritual worlds.

We all want to get away from the rules, regulations, and established orders. The way that it can be done is by becoming a spiritual traveller and being free to move anywhere within the whole body of the supreme being. This is the truth that we seek here and now.

Damkarh

Banjani Ji is another Master who is teaching here, but only to the privileged or advance students on this path. This hidden spiritual city is called Faqiti, Damkarh, which is situated in the Gobi Desert. It lies between the highlands of Mongolia and China. During my first visit, Banjani Ji and I were standing outside the temple. I noticed that the surrounding area was very dusty, as it happens in dry seasons in India. Damkarh is another outpost of this universe and is controlled by the Yellow Hat Lamas.

It is a large and beautiful city representing the activity of the earth religions. It has splendid cathedrals and holy places where we go to study in Satsang while asleep. Banjani Ji is medium height, about five feet seven inches tall. He has brown Indian skin and long hair combed back very neatly. His beard is a mix of black and grey, as is his hair. He has a special spark in his eyes, and it is beyond belief how he expresses the spiritual message through his eyes, known as the Master's Gaze. The expressions in his eyes convey messages very clearly to the Seeker.

Shambhala

It is place of peace. At present, this spiritual city is embedded in the ice of the glacier and peaks about twenty-five thousand feet high at one time or in my early days. A few thousand years back, this used to be flat land in the Eastern Himalaya Mountains inside North Tibet. It is near the Gurla Mandhata Peak, which is the highest. This invisible city is the headquarters of White Brotherhood and is involved in spiritual governing of this world to bring peace. It is also known as the forbidden land. It is believed that Hindus' original religious books have connections here.

Rahakajah

It is known to us in legend as Camelot during the days of King Arthur. It lies in the south-west tip of England near the seaside of Cornwall. It is the home of the Order of the Golden Dawn, a group of Brown Robe Monks. The purpose of this spiritual city is to be the centre for magical forces of this world. At sunset, some people have claimed to see the mirage image of a spiritual city. To the physical eyes, at present this place is abandoned shipyard docklands.

Satdhama

It is situated in the Pyrenees Mountains approximately 11,000 feet high in north-eastern Spain. It is on the border of France and Spain. You will notice all these spiritual cities are in hidden places. Its inhabitants are called the Tulstan Order of the Ancient Brotherhood, but often we hear of them simply as the Brown Robe Monks. They are responsible for the healing purposes in the physical world and other planets of this universe. These mountains are very peaceful and full of wildlife.

Akeveez

It lies in the highlands of southern Guatemala, Central America. The local name is Altos, which means highlands. It is the most beautiful mountainous area, volcanic with clear lakes. There are very few spiritual travellers who are still connected with this five-thousand-year-old civilisation, the Mayans, which is the link between it and the present world. They are known as the Brothers of the Black Robes.

Kimta-Vedah

This city is located in South America on the western border of Venezuela and Columbia, in some of the highest parts of the Andes. At present, there are a lot of disputes between these two countries for border crossing. It is one of the most outstanding stations which the spiritual travellers have established, other than Agam-Des. The purpose of their existence here is to keep watch over the planetary spirits and make sure all is running smoothly here. They are often called the Order of the Green Robes.

Naampak

This is another spiritual city, known as the legendary Rwenjura Mountains of the Moon, in the Republic of Congo in East Africa. This name was given because when viewed from the sky, it appears as two semicircles, like moons. It is very close to the source of the River Nile, and it's a very peaceful place comparable to heaven on earth. It is not to be seen by physical eyes, although it is the home of great spiritual travellers, who are responsible for the care of souls that leave the body at the time of death, especially those who have no one to help them to cross the borders of life and death. They also take care of lost souls due to accidental deaths.

Mumsakah

It is in the southern part of old Georgia, near Russia, hidden away from the eyes of the non-believers. It is in one of the coldest places of the Caucasus Mountains, approximately 18,500 feet high. This region lies between the Black Sea (west) and the Caspian Sea (east). Here, situated in one of the remote areas of the world, lives the Watchers of the Path, who are the protectors of the mind of man. They try to lead our spiritual minds towards God.

Zejirath

It is located near the ruins of Memphis, the temple city of the Egyptians which went underground over five thousand years ago. This used to be a very powerful and beautiful city. Egyptians believe there are many hidden cult temples. Here we find the old faith of that nation, which worships the mysteries of Osiris because these travellers keep faith with the religions and mysteries of the ancient world. They are the keepers of the ancient truths. They were responsible for the pyramids and their positions.

Golden Temples

First Temple: It is located in northern Tibet, hidden deeply in the Thanglha Mountains. It is called Katsu-pari Monastery and is under the supervision of Fubi Kants. At present, Kants is eleven hundred years old and is about five feet nine inches tall as far as I could judge while standing in front of him. He has a dark maroon robe, and he sometimes wears a turban of the same colour; sometimes he wears pure white clothes. Part one of the golden book is in this white marble temple. This is where many students are taken to study during their dream state, when they have joined "The Way to God".

Second Temple: In this physical world, it is at Agam-Desh, the spiritual city in the remote Hindu Kush Mountains, near the Afghanistan and Kashmir border in central Asia. Alexander the Great crossed the Hindu Kush Mountains during 329 BC in this area to enter old Punjab, now Pakistan. This temple is called Garreh-Hira and is under the supervision of Yabal Sakabi. He is believed to be over five thousand years old. His appearance is a bald head, dark eyes, dark gold skin, and a pleasant smile.

I can say he is about my height. He wears a maroon robe and a rope belt around his waist. Students sit on large rugs when attending classes in the hall. "Sometimes I wonder how old these rugs will be? It has a platform in the back where the Master stands and Seekers listen. Here upon an altar is the second golden book. Some other details of this place are mentioned in my book *The Will of God*.

Third Temple: It is in the city of Retz on the planet Venus. It is called the House of Moksh. This temple is similar to an old English cathedral in London. There is a podium from which Master Rami-Noori gives instructions to the Seekers who are brought there to study. He is the guardian of this section of the third golden book. Master Rami-Nuri is tall and well-built with dark eyes and a square face.

Fourth Temple: It is in the astral plane. This temple sits in the middle of a green park in the heart of the astral plane's capital city, Sahasra-Dal-Kanwal. The guardian of this temple is Gopal Das. He is from Egypt, but his name is similar to Hindu Indians. The name Gopala refers to Lord Krishna. He has European look and has blue eyes. His hair is a somewhat golden colour and is shoulder length.

He wears the maroon robe, sometimes he wears white colours as well. This temple is an octagon building of red and white sandstone. It is in the park with eight walkways leading to the centre of this mostly round hall. There is a spheroid mineral block on which is placed the fourth golden book.

Fifth Temple: The Temple of Sakapuri is on the causal plane. It is under the supervision of a Sufi Master, Shams Mohammad of Tabrizi (Iran), who also was the Master of the poet Rumi. He is broad and is heaviest in figure when appearing to anyone on this plane. He usually wears a dark maroon cloak, has long dark hair, wears a turban, and sometimes wears white clothes. His eyes are deep brown, and he has brown skin similar to Indian or Pakistan origin. He had a very historical relationship with the sun.

During his days on earth, once everyone ignored him or boycotted him to not give fire so he could cook his food, he looked at the sun and said, "You are Sun, and so am I. If you are my friend, provide your heat to my food so that it is cooked." It is believed the sun lowered itself till his food was cooked. The fifth golden book is encased in a wide but short glass-type casing. It is on a stand where a soft light shines softly upon its open pages. Once you read one page, the next page will turn itself for you to read.

Sixth Temple: It is on the mental plane, in the city of Mer-Kailasha. The guardian of this golden book is Japanese Master Sato Kuraj, who was a regular visitor to Sri Darwin Ji. He is small but has a very cute smile on his face when appearing to Seekers. It appears very much like the ancient Temple of Diana, which was at a city on the coast of Turkey. This temple is built in the Greek style, and within it is a long, flat block on which rests the sixth golden book.

Seventh Temple: It is in the city of Arhirit, on the etheric plane, and is under the supervision of Chinese Master Lai Tasie, who spent most of his life meditating in caves. He is of short height with a long, drooping moustache. His eyes are dark, and he wears a very colourful hat. His mouth is wide but always turned up in a smiling Buddha gesture. The light around him is silvery white and always accompanied by the sound of buzzing bees, and he wears a maroon robe. This building is a great, towering temple with many floors, and inside is placed the seventh golden book.

Soul Plane: Sach-Khand: This temple is called Param-khand, and it is located in the heart of a magnificent park. There is no community-type life similar to lower planes because this is the soul plane. We find this golden temple under the supervision of Master Nirgunna Ekom. He is here to guide us to the first manifestation of God, Satnam Ji, where we find Self-Realisation. Above, there are golden temples and golden books on each plane, which leads us to experience God-Realisation, Anami-Lok, and God itself.

—

HOLY BEGGARS

Beggars are often considered a disgrace to any community or country. These are the people who chose to not work or take any responsibility in life, and they feel no shame in putting out their hands to ask for money. I meet a few who are the victims of circumstances and driven insane by families, and they have lost their pride and accepted the attitude of "Who cares?" In some countries, begging runs in the families, and children are used and trained from a very early age how to beg.

Now, "What hope can we have? That one day they will follow God. The chances are very slim, although they are begging in the name of God. It is very strange when you ponder upon their lifestyle. We hear through the media now and then that one beggar died, and it is found that he had one million pounds in his bank accounts. In India, it has been found that beggars are sometimes multi-millionaires. They don't need to beg, but it has become a habit for them, which they cannot get rid of easily.

There is another kind, and I call them holy beggars. They rob you officially in the name of God, and they have registered charity numbers issued by governments. This is normal practice throughout this world. They are known as saints or priests, and it is a known practice in world religions to ask for 10 percent of earnings from their followers. People love to donate money to their respective cults or religions, taking it as their religious obligation. Religion is a weakness of humans in this world.

While living in this world, people want to belong to some organisation to say who they are: Hindu, Muslim, Christian, or others. Man has failed to find God within, and so he uses the external approach, which seems easy. He makes a pilgrimage to some religious temples, and within these temples are some statues or pictures representing religious prophets. The majority of them know that statues are not Gods, but it gives them this feeling, and they feel blessed.

It is their hope to carry on in life. Everyone needs to be part of some religion or organisation to create an identity and say, "I belong here." Otherwise, they will be lost in wonderland. Very few can stand alone and do something for themselves. Many people do a pilgrimage every year to their respective holy temples. Christians go to Rome, Jerusalem, and other places. Muslims go to Makkah. Hindus have hundreds of temples all over India.

I wish God was living in man-made buildings, but it is not true. Why do you have to travel thousands of miles when God is sitting within yourself all the time? You don't have the time to look within in your very home, but you can find a number of days to travel thousands of miles. All our prophets had expressed throughout their writing that God is within; you simply have to make the effort to experience it. At present, saints are very few, and most religions are led by priest-craft.

They are not saints, and so they fail to convey the correct message of their religious writings. Many priests are employed by their respective religious organisations, and they are trained to ask for donations. All religious TV channels are doing the same. They use these funds to build temples, preach against other religions, or destroy the creations of God. These temples become a regular source of their income, and these priests play lots of mind games within their organisations to squire their own jobs.

These holy beggars are living a luxurious life when you (who donates) live in poverty life. You are the donator, and you do not realise you are the root cause of the destruction to other people or nations. Have you ever realized, what you are doing? Religions are fighting more with other countries than governments. God does not live or reside in temples. Neither is it asking for man-made money. I was watching the Indian news on 15 June 2013, and the Kedarnath Dham (a temple) in Uttarakhand and so many other temples.

They were totally drowned and destroyed by heavy rain, with thousands of corpses lying everywhere. That proves my point written at the beginning of this paragraph. Religions are similar to the crawling of a child. The ultimate goal is God, and you can only experience it when you start to walk. The majority of priest-craft, although they are claiming to be religious, are most likely politically motivated. These temples become indirectly political platforms.

Religious followers come to pray, but they become political pawns as voters because their priest or forefront saint said so. Often these saints recommend, guide, or sometimes dictate to the followers to vote for some particular party. Once the majority of political leaders are elected, they are supposed to run the country. Instead, they come and sit beside some saint's feet for their win and success. If this saint was capable of doing this, then this saint should be campaigning for his position in Parliament.

Asian saints know that they are capable of doing nothing, and so they take full advantage of these people's belief. People should not vote for these candidates, who in turn are relying on these holy beggars. How can they help you or run your country? Beware—all your actions are counted for karma.

IMPORTANCE OF TIME

Time is a unit of measurement to calculate the past, present, and future. Without this unit, all the events will pass without any recording of their presence. Time is our educational factor; otherwise, day and night will appear, but we would not know what took place at what time. With Greenwich Mean Time, we can know the time all through this world. It is the average taken from the rotation of the earth from noon to noon. We normally take one complete day as twenty-four hours.

Time varies in each country because all the countries cannot face the sun at the same time. Twenty-four hours turn into months, years, decades, centuries, millennia, and Yugas. Astrologers divide these into number of cycles, as described in the chapter on the physical universe. Planets orbit the sun at different speeds, distances, and positions, and they affect humans to bring good luck and good health. There is one principle that supersedes all these effects, and that is karma.

If we create good karma, then it does not matter where these planets are. You will have good luck throughout as the positions of these planets turn in your favour. We often pray and say, "Please, God, forgive me. Help me look after my children and family. Save my job." The list is endless. Do not ask God or the Master for forgiveness. I will stress this point very strongly. Forgive yourself so that you don't create any further bad karma.

Otherwise, newly created karma will turn into many folds and will knock on your door, and asking you to face it. Who is responsible for all this? That is only one person: yourself. When you are facing this payment that is known as "I am going through bad times", of course you are—but for how long will depend on your creation and the way the payment is being made. We never recognise this as our fault and always try to blame others.

How long does it take to clear particular karma? It becomes a cycle measured in years. During this payment, you are caught in a catch-22 when you are trying to make a payment, but this chaos situation pushes you into creating many more, and it becomes a never-ending circle or wheel of eighty-four. This is where you need a spiritual Master to lead you out of this mess. He is also limited because he is here to provide guidance and to point out the action required, but putting the things right is your responsibility.

The majority of the Seekers are taking years to decide. When you do decide to sort out everything, it is possible you are already walking towards a depression state. Many times, we lose our faith in Spirit or the Master, saying the Master did not help. God can wipe out every soul's bad karma, bad health, negative situations, and poverty in a split second. However, then all purpose of schooling is lost for the souls. The Master can do the same, but you will never learn the lessons. This is where all the religions fail in this world.

They are purposely leading the followers into prayers; in my terminology, it is begging for everything. If I am asking everyone to not beg, that means I am of a strong character as a person. So, what is your problem? Why can't you be like me? By begging, you lose your self-respect, and in this world, you will be kicked about everywhere. Why are you praying to God, the Master, or statues when God has given you everything equally because it possesses you?

It only wants you to realise, become aware of it' presence, and have all you desire. When you come to this condition of living, all your desires vanish. If you want to carry on suffering, that is your free will to do so, and I wish you all the best in your sufferings. Turn the clock around and begin to work around your situations. When these bad karmas know that you are knocking at their door, they begin to disappear, and your time changes in your favour.

It is only by giving up everything that one gains reality in God. If you care for nothing, you are detaching from worldly things, and you will receive the gifts from God. Whoever gives all to God receives all from God, and you become the assistant. This is why I have been stressing my point many times that learn to give instead of receiving. Every second counts. Emotional love leads to attachment, you become a very weak person, and your bad time starts.

Our whole lives are involved around this factor known as time. In the lower worlds, it is matter, energy, space, and time. Your time in this world begins even before you realise the importance of it. In the womb, you don't know who you are, but your mum and dad start counting the months for your arrival in this world. Your time and date are noted to mark your arrival in this world. Then it is your first birthday, then teen years, and soon you are declared an adult.

Graduation, marriage, going to work and coming home on time, retirement, and even your death—the total number of years are noted to mark your departure. Now you see your whole life is based or tied to one factor: Time. Despite knowing the importance of time, we waste half of our lives doing nothing. Most people love their sleep, and some have plenty of time to go to the pub for drinking. Ladies have plenty of time to gossip.

Although at times it can be very entertaining, the question is, "What is your spiritual gain out of this?" Other times are wasted on arguments, fighting, and jealousy to stop the other person from doing any good.

Despite my effort on many occasions to point out the importance of time, Seekers are still on the same railway track. As long as you are glued to your old lifestyle tracks, you will never be happy or progress on a spiritual basis. You want to see the whole eternity in a split second of your thoughts, but what are you doing to materialise your goal?

Time is one of the main factors in this world which dictates our lives. The sun and moon follow time to let us know that it is day or night. Clouds act as a shield to prevent sunshine on earth. The earth is always on the move to reach its destiny to see the face of the sun. Can you relate your life to this example? All the stars shine in our galaxy, and we admire their beauty. Are you shining like them? Why don't you shine so that others can admire you?

Time is so important and short in this life. Most of the time, we are living or base our lives on our dreams. Dreams alone are not enough. Try to materialise them; otherwise there is no success. Why our dreams do not materialise because we do not base our lives on the basis of the will of God, we often request God to act according to our will. That is when you are praying for worthless things or situations. Mainly there are three types of people living in this world.

First are those always behind in schedules of work or life. They are always late. These are the people who make the worst use of their time, and I call them the failure type. They will never succeed in their dream projects. Don't be surprised to learn that these people dream the most but fail to execute them.

Second are the people who know the value of time but simply manage with their daily routines, and they can manage to materialise some of their dreams. This means if they can't gain much, they haven't lost either. But you need to do more to achieve that plus element.

Third are the most successful people in life. They have the ability to project into the future, and they are fully prepared to face new challenges. They put the past experience to good use in the present, and they are in full command. They are very wise people. This is why they are sitting in the chair as our leaders. The leadership could be in business, politics, or spirituality, and people often go to them for advice. You could be this person if you act now.

There's another kind. There are some who go beyond these classes of people. They have achieved all and now are in control of their time. They spend their time and breathe air as they wish to do. They roam free beyond human knowing and control their destiny. The past can be used to learn and be put to good use to enjoy the present moment. Live in the present moment, otherwise there will be so many tomorrows, and you will never catch a tomorrow.

Past and future always give you pain. The past has already gone, and you cannot relive it. The future is out of your reach yet. When you do reach into the future, at that moment it will be present, so why do we wait for the future when you are already here? When you are happy, it is not wasted time. In happiness, you create good karma added to your final accounts. Time is a gift from God. Use it wisely. Once you have lost it or wasted it, there is no recovery.

There are four seasons of the year in our physical universe. All the seasons are timed for our physical well-being so that the soul can experience without any problem, because the physical body is very important for the soul. As the present moment, change into minutes, hours, months, and years. Make sure that you have grown spiritually. Time spent laughing without any purpose or plan is wasted, and at the same time, it is another day nearer to the grave. Awake spiritually, and then you will choose your day.

In the olden days, every day was our present day because there was no counting in numbers. There was no recognition of past or future. All religions recognised one particular day as their favourite. For example, it is Friday for Islam, Sunday for Christians, and Thursday for black magicians.

Some consider Wednesday as their lucky day, and other days are used for different beliefs. If we remove name tags such as Monday to Sunday, then all days will be the same and lucky. This illusion is self-created by us.

As our minds progressed, these numbers or names of days became part of the human educational system, and we created seven days per week and four weeks in one month. According to the old calendar there were thirteen months per year (365 / 28 = 13). Then the realisation came that each month varied in comparison to our natural four seasons. That was the reason to alter the numbers of days in each month, such as 30, 31, 28, and 29 days every leap year to accommodate our longest day on 21 June and our shortest day on 21 December.

Because of these calculations, all four seasons come in similar months and are accommodated within 365 days. If we study further, at present these four seasons appear on similar dates every year, but the names of days change. There is a time cycle of years when the same day and dates repeat themselves as well. This pattern is sometimes five, six, or eleven years, and leap year repeats itself every twenty-eight years.

Hold on to any happy moment you had in the past because it can help you at present to be close to God. Most of the time, we are living other people's lives, either due to sincerity, obligation, fear, or duty. By the time you become aware of yourself, who are you? Your own time is up. Do whatever you need to do, but always do it in the name of God so that all your actions turn into good karma. That way, every action of yours becomes creative, and time is spent wisely.

Every moment brings change in our lives and experiences so that the present moment does not mean you are standing still and doing nothing. The reason for listening to other people's dictates is a sign of bad karma. Turn the table around and begin to gain good karma. Be in command of your life as a Master of your own universe. The time of your life is very limited, so it must be planned what to be done and when. What is time? It is an experience. Make sure it is not wasted and experience.

It is gained physically and spiritually for your own benefit and for the good of the whole, so that the others can learn something under your umbrella. The present moment is continuous of is-ness. It is like a drop of rain, which disappears in the sand right in front of your eyes while you are deciding what to do with it. If we manage to take care of our present moment, then the future will take care of itself. Since I was young, I knew time was very important, and so I planned my life as to where I should be and at what age.

As far as I am concerned, I achieved my spiritual goal at the age of twenty-eight years. It did not materialise the way I wanted to see; that was beyond my control. As they say, better late than never, so here I am today. When I became aware that my spiritual goal was not materialising the way it should have been, then I set up another goal on the physical basis. I must pack up my working tools at the age of fifty years so that I could spend all my time in the presence of God.

I worked very hard, and with the help of Spirit, I accomplished this goal at the age of forty-seven years. I did not hesitate for a day to pack up my working tools. Time is very important. Make plans as you go along, or else you will never see the face of God. A majority of the people are saying, "Just forget about God. You will not even see the face of God's angel." So far, if you have not realised the value of time, it simply means you have not discovered life, and this is the reason for your suffering at present.

Although the present moment is one, you can create two out of one if you know how to experience it wisely. That means organised time is time earned; otherwise, it is all wasted. Time is a great healer, and whatever came your way as a bad experience will be gone tomorrow. Be the silent soldier of God, who is waiting for you to be its assistant. Desires are known for our sufferings. We spend half of our lives planning to execute our desires. If we begin to act now, we can materialise half of them in no time.

Don't daydream—plan and act. The majority of our members are not working, and as for living, so they have twenty-four hours for themselves, yet nothing materialising, you should ask the question to your inner self: Why? Do you know every today is tomorrow for yesterday? So why worry about your past? Leave the past behind and move on with your life. The flowers are ready to bloom in your life. If you have read my book *The Will of God*, you'll know I have left my past behind long ago.

You can imagine the life situation I could have been at present, physically as well as mentally. I moved on with the present moment by saying, "Who cares?" That is why I am laughing today. Time is slow for those who wait at the seashore. Time is far too long for those who grieve and far too short for those who are happy and enjoying the eternity. For those who are happy, Christmas is coming soon, and last Christmas seems like it was yesterday. Time goes so fast. For those who grieve every moment, A day is like a span of one year.

I am not simply giving you advice—I personally have been through every single problem of yours, so you'd better act and improve life. All moments of life should be lived because they are coins of gold. You are also golden, and your destiny to be reached is also the land of gold. Your creator is waiting for you at the golden temple so that you can receive the word of gold in the presence of the golden man, the first personification of God. When you know you are wanted and waited upon, do you have time?

My love and Spirit always surround you.

KAL POWER

What is Kal power? It is negative energy within. Kal power is the main issue discussed in all world religions or scriptures. Kal is the negative pole, and it is equal and opposite to positive, so it is as important as positive. The whole theory of the lower worlds is based on equal and opposite. Without Kal, nothing can exist. We often don't want to face Kal. This is also Kal because you are holding a negative attitude. If there is no night, day will carry on forever.

You may think that will be a good idea, but at the end it will become destructive for the whole universe because the growth atoms in this world will become less and less with time. Kal, or negativity, is as important in our lives as positivity. Kal is often looked at as an enemy prospect. I heard remarks from so many. "Yes, I was OK—till Kal power intervened and my life became hell." Is it really? People with these thoughts are believed to be very religious, but I don't think they are following their respective teachings.

If their respective teachings are stressing the same view, then I will say their religious scriptures and their founders or prophets had never been above the mental plane. The true picture can only be seen when you go into the soul plane and above, and you view the lower worlds from there. Now you will see both sides of the weighing scale. If there is only one side of the scale, this scale will not go up or down. If nothing moves in this world, what will be the outcome?

The rising of smoke is as important as the law of gravity. Can you imagine if we threw something in the air, and it suspended itself there? I am sure you get the importance of equal and opposite. We all want to be positive or lead positive and progressive lives, but to achieve this, we often choose routes of negativity for our progress. What we create during this process will be beyond our control. We are often faced with hatred, jealousy, theft, and backstabbing on our part or with the people around us.

Our own creations are responsible for suffering. What is Kal? We often blame Kal for our failures. It is not Kal that is responsible for all this. These are our self-created situations or conditions and our own weaknesses. When we have to face them, we often blame Kal for this. Kal is only responsible for reminding us of our weaknesses.

We all have five passions within us, and we let them run wild. We are responsible for most of our creations and sufferings. The combination of five passions can also be called Kal, but at the same time God gave us other qualities known as Chitta, Manas, Buddhi, and Ahankar to judge and execute our actions. We can judge and execute all our actions as we go along in life.

God has given us three **gunas,** or **virtues,** as well.

Tamas: is the state of darkness or materiality

Rajas: is the state of energy, action, and passion

Sattva: is a state of harmony, balance, joy, intelligence, purity, and goodness

God gave us another **five virtues** to protect us from other wrong-doings.

Viveka: how to discriminate from wrong and right

Kshama: how to tolerate and forgive others

Santosha: contentment; this protects us from excessive greed

Vairaag: detachment; protection or the opposite to Moha

Dinta: humility; the opposite to vanity or Ahankar

We have five passions to lead us astray or create wrong-doings, and we also have good qualities within to balance our wrong-doings—but we often fail to use them. We all are individuals, and if we act that way, we can control our actions, but we don't see ourselves that way. We become part of the masses and enter the rat race. All our religions are mass based, and you are part of that crowd; and you do what others are doing. It never occurs to you whether it is right or wrong.

All religions are the main cause of our failures or sufferings. We are often looking for solutions to problems through our religious principles. The action and reaction of our five passions and our virtues will land each individual in Kriyaman karma (daily karma) and Prarabdh (known as fate karma). Our lives or sufferings are based on that, which is totally our own creation. Many also blame others for doing black magic on them when there is little truth in it.

Brahma is the overall lord of the lower planes, and the king of the dead is the accountant of our total karma. If we are responsible for creating karma, then Dharam-raj's accounts will create situations, or they happen naturally to make sure we pay back what we have created. He does not spare anyone. The lower worlds are a training ground for souls via creation, worlds, situations, and five passions, so you are bound to create karma.

This creation and paying back is our suffering and learning for the soul. Kal, or Brahm, makes sure you have gone through every experience possible and explored all negative and positive situations to be a properly balanced person. Kal is the teacher, and you are the student. The sooner

114

you learn this, the sooner life becomes calm and easy to live. For every situation we go through, we are aware that it is for some purpose, and we face it with a smile.

The situation disappears quickly with experience in our account. People with positive or spiritual minds guide others to create good karma in order to eliminate the negative and to lead balanced lives. One day you will be a spiritual human to guide others. Many blame God for our sufferings. God is our father and creator, so how do you expect your own father to punish you? Do you as the parent punish your children? The answer is within. Create good karma. Kal will help you to learn as a good friend.

Tell others what Kal is. Learn to face the challenges. Kal will be smiling with you, and God will bless you because you are ready to be a assistant in the spiritual worlds. Once you understand Kal, life will be much easier. If you suffer at the hands of others, they are under the influence of five passions and do the worst they possibly can. Their negative actions or deeds are recorded by the lord of karma. Have patience; they will suffer too.

Lots of people purposely did wrong against me, and I suffered, but after many years they are suffering now, whereas I am still around. Kal and positive are both silent; we awake them with our knowingness. Children are so innocent and don't know what Kal or positive is, but they are always smiling. Do you know the majority of children up to the age of three cannot lie? As an experiment, purposely tell them to not touch something in your absence.

When you come back, ask them if they touched what you told them not to. If they touched it, the response will be, "Yes, I have." At the age of four, their answer most likely will be the opposite. With age, these passions wake up within. It's very similar to a meditation practitioner who tries to wake up Kundalini to achieve psychic powers. With age, we awake Kal within to achieve worldly goods and status. This power leads us to the world of destruction.

Europe is a lot better place to live when compared to Third World countries; people in these countries are suffering for many reasons, the living standard is very low, and there are water and food problems. Kal is not after anyone to make people suffer. It is yourself, and others are after each other to achieve or deceive. Kal is only recording your actions; the reactions will appear later. Many times, someone said to me, "Kal attacked," or, "Kal is after me."

Kal is not a ghost who is trying to track you down. You are Kal yourself. When acting negative for the others, if you are in fear due to that, you are Kal too. We all act as Kal to each other, whether knowingly or unknowingly. Each person is frustrated from different angles, so each person is more interested in looking for remedies to their problems, and during that we do lot of wrongful acts as well.

Kal is a good friend, but only if you know it.

———

MASTERS & SEEKERS

We all are the creation of God, but if there is any first Master, that is Satnam Ji. He is the first personification of God. He is the powerhouse for God. He sits between the infinite and the creation of God, and he is responsible for all souls. He resides in the soul plane, appears in human form, and looks like an American Indian: golden bronzed, shaven head, muscular, and about forty years old. He wears bracelets on his upper arms.

In his presence, everything appears in a golden shade, and he sits upon a huge jewelled lotus with folded arms. He is always in meditation. The Master is responsible for materialising Seekers' set-up spiritual goals. Many Seekers are very serious, and others take everything very lightly. At the same time, they expect heaven to open up for them. It has been learnt over the years if any Master is too much of the disciplinary, the Seekers begin to leave him. Because all Seekers want a Master to take full care of them while they can have fun.

All religious pilgrimages to their respective temples are based on this theme. We all pray to God so that our desires are fulfilled, but when all our situations are normal or pleasing, we often forget God and do not feel the necessity to pray. The first knowingness is that you are soul, and it is to free soul from the lower worlds, whereas before you have been fulfilling the needs of the physical body, which is temporary and dies after its given life span. This life is a continual succession of spiritual opportunities, but we often fail to grab them.

Discipline and spiritual thoughts are the main contributors to having spiritual success. All Seekers cannot become proper spiritual travellers because of a lack of discipline and hardly any seriousness in the teachings they are following. In the same way, it is good to be born in any religion, but spiritually it's not very healthy to remain there. It is good to be born a child, but it's bad to stay like a child for all your life. To be a assistant of God, spiritual awakening and taking responsibility for each action is a must.

The Seeker must face his or her weaknesses and conquer them one by one to bring a spiritual life in balance. You must lead an ethical life similar to your Master, or as expected by your teachings. Be an example to the others. Spirit only enters into pure hearts so that the truth can be revealed. God resides in each soul as state of consciousness, but some Seekers are so pure in their hearts that God uses them as a platform or as assistants. It is your set goal and responsibility.

As Jesus said, once you put hands upon the plough handles, there is no turning back. The Master said perfection can be given to any Seeker within a matter of seconds. A word in the ear is enough provided the Seeker can grasp and act upon it, but the Seeker often fails to maintain his or her state of consciousness. You must learn to stand back so that divine Spirit can work through you. Spirit can be experienced live within yourself, and that will be your achievement. In order to experience this, you must have a calm and untroubled mind.

Qualities of the Master

He holds a much higher state of consciousness at the inner, and his outer actions are always in the name of God. The Master's will, is the will of God. Most of the time, he is dwelling in the beingness state, the worlds of pure Spirit. There is no religion, no doors to open, and nowhere to go—It Just Is. When the Master gains master-ship, he attains consciousness with God, and from there all his actions are under the direction of Spirit. He will never be interested in establishing a new religion. This point is easier said than done.

The Master is not a healer, and neither does he pose as one, but the whole world believes it through mythological stories. That is why people often request healings. Seekers lose the true purpose of following. The Master always rejects any kind of violence. The Master does not obey man-made laws, and neither does he break any while living on earth because he is law unto himself. His approach to all creation is very universal. He is not for or against any colour, race of people, or religion.

He loves all because God does so on neutral grounds. He is full of love and good health because any person with a disability cannot become a real spiritual Master. He is not a slave to anyone, and he asks no favour of any man. He always pays for what he gets, and he creates his own living by doing suitable jobs. Spiritually, he is not allowed to live on donations given by followers or funds of any organisation. If he does, he cannot be the living Master of the time.

He only sleeps three or four hours daily and can manage to work twenty-four hours without fatigue. Religious leaders operate differently because their base is the social system, gathering and praying to seek everything free. These religious systems teach people how to pray, when actually "Man is a God" clothed in rags but is the Master of the universe going about material gains, which are for temporary use. Each religious follower is happy to remain within a self-created prison.

The Master may not be educated in a university or college, but he has gone through severe spiritual disciplines or tests, which are far more superior or harder than any education. He does not interfere in the consciousness of any person unless asked, and neither he allow any Seeker to lean upon him because otherwise, the Seeker will never become a Master of his own universe. This is why when the Master has shown the spiritual way to the Seeker, then the Seeker must walk alone.

The Master can do Akashic or soul readings for any Seeker, but it serves no purpose for any spiritual advancement. We should be concerned only with the present moment or the continuous is-ness. When a Seeker's biggest interest is to gain knowledge of past lives and have some excitement, or to know if he has held important positions in previous lives, these are mind-pleasing games, and the true purpose of following is lost. The future can be forecasted, but that is based on your previous karma.

It is better to start building a strong foundation today, for future happy living. Aura adjustment or balancing is another fraud business. Your aura is based on your karma, good or bad, which is reflected or surrounds your body, can any person wipe out your karma? Those who do claim are very deceptive people. It is the craving within for spiritual knowledge or about God that leads you to become a Seeker.

We have followed all religious beliefs and try to memorise all religious verses, but nothing leads to spiritual awakening other than surface knowledge. One day you will realise it does not matter how serious you have been; it did not lead you to any significant achievement. Most religions don't believe in having a living Master, but they have full faith in the Master who was here five or ten thousand years ago.

These Masters have done their respective duties at that time and have already incarnated a few times in other countries, but we still believe they are around. All these ascended Masters have little say in the physical plane. It is similar to that deceased doctor who cannot treat a sick man, or a deceased mother who cannot provide milk for her own child. If departed Masters could take care of new Seekers, then there is no need for any new Masters on the physical plane.

God needs one clear channel all the time, and this is why so many Masters appeared time after time—and they will continue to do so. A Seeker in the body must have a Master in the physical body that is the fixed law. That applies to any educational system. Any request made to a departed Master in the hope that he will help you will be disappointed because in order to please you, he is not going to use lower powers or take physical form.

Neither is he able to because he has incarnated somewhere else. True Masters always pass their spiritual mantle to the new, worthy soul in physical form. Living and being stuck in the past is our failure point. The modern mind, do not believe in the living Master but finds no difficulty in accepting the story of past Masters who lived a few centuries back. I wonder sometimes what education they had, given that they cannot analyse this simple truth. The living Master of the time will not ask or guide you to go on any pilgrimage to find or seek God.

God exists within each soul as a state of consciousness. The Master guides you to sit wherever you are and meditate within to spiritually awake yourself. There is nothing that you cannot know or understand. All spiritual knowingness and spiritual planes are at your disposal. You are the reflection of big mirror, and there is nothing that you cannot see. In the same way, you see your reflection in the river of God. You will glide like a hawk in the sky upon the currents of Spirit as a free soul, and that will be your awareness because you are part of God.

The more you become aware of the light of God within, the more you know that you are part of God, and the humbler you become to God's creation. This is the result of self-surrender to the Master, Spirit, and God. It was your decision to live spiritually free and not in a self-created prison. This is the reason why God created lower worlds and reincarnation systems to explore the whirlpool, so that we can learn and one day become assistants in the cause of God.

A true satguru is appointed by the supreme deity, known as Satnam Ji, because the present Master has earned the authority to wear the spiritual mantle. He speaks with authority and he maintains his state of God consciousness. Regardless of his state of consciousness, many Seekers believe that the Master is free from physical problems or psychic harm or disease. This is not true. As long as he is living in the lower worlds, he is bound to suffer just like us.

These are **four** stages of spiritual following by the **Seekers.**

Those who are excited by the spiritual writings but fail to practice.

Those who listen to the Master and read the discourses but are mentally restless.

Those who follow the Master and his teachings but still fail to reach a set goal.

Those who are successful and are travelling within—but these are very few.

The majority of them are stuck in the problem zone. No man has managed to solve the problems of life by following any religion or philosophy. It is the realisation of responsibility to clear any negative karma earned already, and now he is making his own way in life, earning his own keep and not living off others as he used to do. The Master is there to guide you all the time, and he is very happy with those who are walking along, but he does not look back at who is following or not.

This decision is left with the Seeker and is known as free will. God has granted free will to all souls to learn according to their own pace. The Master is interested only in the spiritual welfare of the Seeker to make sure he makes his own castle in heaven. The Master is not interested in self-created problems of any Seeker; This is exactly what he is pointing at to take responsibility of each karma created. The majority of humans are thieves at heart, and they will try to get away with whatever they can.

It is the fear of law, not of facing imprisonment that makes them stay within the boundaries of a safe zone or maintain their good status in society. We are not here in any winning or losing position or for austere practices to eliminate these karmas. As we unfold all of our doings, we balance our karmas. We should pay full attention to health of the body and the mind. The Way to God's teachings are beyond religion and so we cannot sell any material goods such as jewellery, flashy posters, uniforms, or anything that all religions are doing.

On the same basis, we do not celebrate the deaths or births of our past Masters. We believe in the present moment and the present Master. All religions are based on past moments, repeating old mythological stories. During that process, they have forgotten how to enjoy present moment, and they cannot dream of what the future holds for them. All our Masters live in this moment, and this is why they do not hold strong human relations. I can sit alone forever, and probably I'll be more-happier if left alone.

All physical conversations force me to act as a normal human. Sometimes I do feel irritated because of this lost time. No Seeker can serve two Masters and gain any spiritual grounds. The semantics of two Masters are different, and this will act as split attention of the Seeker. That cannot be spiritually beneficial. All Seekers must give their current mailing address if they want to receive teachings, not their relatives' address.

This is not a good practice because if we allow this, we would be as guilty as the Seeker. This indicates we are not being honest. Many people do this because of certain circumstances in the family and some fear running in their minds. We cannot progress spiritually with fear in the mind and dishonesty with yourself and the Master. The Master does not allow anyone to pray for others or to change their state of consciousness. We must grant psychic space or free will to all.

More harm is done through prayers to others and yourself without the permission of the person. Many people try to harm the Master or any spiritual person, and these souls are living within the protection shield of Spirit. The cosmic Spirit is a law unto itself, and so whatever comes, it automatically reflects or goes back to the sender. The sender suffers the consequences and is responsible for self-created negative actions. Masters are laws unto themselves, and they are only responsible to God.

The main failure point of Seekers is that they try to seek as much knowledge as possible. That is the requirement for the mind. However, success only comes when you stop seeking and stop clinging to any materialistic thought. All universes are the temple of Spirit, and Seekers are its sanctuary. Go within—there is nothing you cannot know or understand. Do you know that as you progress spiritually, your facial features begin to change as well?

Self-surrender is very important to the Master and God. The secret of self-surrender is this: be so completely interested in the Master that nothing else matters. Let this faith grow as you and the Master are one, walking and talking all the time. The Master will take care of your all required securities. Once you are in harmony with Spirit, all your problems begin to solve, and all requests are answered without fail. Your will-power is getting stronger by day, and with strong will-power, you can move mountains.

Your will-power will also begin to go along with divine will, and now you are a microcosm reflecting the macrocosm. The creed of "The Way to God" is that all life flows from God downwards to the worlds below, and nothing can exist without the will of God. The existence of God is only proven to those who make the effort and live in the higher states of consciousness all the time, but it cannot be proven to non-believers.

Masters of this path are against the use of artificial drugs, hypnosis, yoga, or any other means to have self-deceiving experiences. The Way to God is the key to spiritual freedom, and it's the key to heaven. Unless you are born again, you cannot see the kingdom of God. Complete transformation from a physical being to a spiritual being is required to have this experience. The Seeker must learn to live on the minimum physical needs.

He can live on a minimum amount of food because his intake will be Spirit. Most of his leisure time is spent in meditation. With spiritual success, the Seeker must be at peace within; if not, he cannot bring peace to others. A Seeker's success is the success of the Master, and it has been worth the effort of the Master to discipline the Seeker.

QUOTATIONS

To believe in God is strength.
To believe in religion is weakness.
To believe in politics is Kal.

God is one; religions are many.
So are their struggles.

Physical-Realisation: when your birth is acknowledged.
Self-Realisation: when you know you are a soul.
God-Realisation: when you know how God operates.

Being alone is strength.
Being in a group is weakness.
Being lonely is depression.

All humans are karmic sick but don't know how to heal themselves.
The Master shows the way, but they follow not.
Yet they claim to be the Seekers.

Life is based on fairy-tale stories.
You'd better learn to face reality.
Those people who cannot control
Their emotions often fail in life.

All religious scriptures are correct and lead the individual to God.
It is the wrong interpretation of scholars,
Or it's not understood by the followers, that leads them to Kal.

There is land and sky. In between are your passions.
They will take you down under or to God.

The one who is, has no name.
The one who has a name, is not God.

Freedom is to live life on your conditions.
Spiritual freedom is to walk away from this
With your own free will.

You can experience God's worlds while still living.
Religions are pointing to this meeting after death,
To which there is no proof.

Those who recite too many verses
Are depending on religious words
But not God.

Those who follow religion are not religious.
I do not follow any religion, but I am religious.

Don't engrave your goals in sand; one tide comes, and all vanish,
Engrave your goals on a solid base so that nothing can shake it.
Positive attitude and strong will-power create miracles.

If we remove money and politics all religions will,
Always remain in Satya-Yuga.
As long as money and politics are involved,
It is no longer religion, it is a battleground for ownership.

We all want God in our lives. We are more interested in,
Looking for remedies to our problems, but not to God.

To know God, the biggest obstacle
In the way of true Seeker is
Failing to walk away from religion.

Do not thump your foot on ground.
Float like angels in the sky.
Your destiny is not far away.

Pray for something, and hope to materialise—
Both are like dreams to which you cannot rely on.
Actions speak louder than words.

Duniya which kamyaab hone vaste, loka naal jurhna jarurri hai,
Sadh bannan vaste, loka nu torhna jarurri hai. (Punjabi)

Rays of light are the evidence of the sun's existence.
Awaken the light within so that others can feel your presence.

Sometimes the critic is
Who cannot tolerate your success.

Those eyes looking at me, evil or with love,
I bless them all, to let them near me.
That is my choice.

Sand needs cement to hold up a building.
Life needs the bondage of love.
Otherwise, both can slip through your fingers,
In no time.

The Master plays all the best, melodious tunes
So that followers can benefit spiritually.
But the Seekers will only accept, like or follow
that which suits them physically.

Prayer to God is never denied;
It depends on what you asked.

129

No person in this world is wrong.
Every person can justify his actions.
People's actions are based on the situation
They are in, or were in.

A religious wave or belief of any Seeker
Is the biggest obstacle in finding the spiritual truth.

You live in light, and the whole world will light up.
You live in darkness, and the whole world will become dark for you.

****

SEEDS OF GOD

Let's take the example of a marigold plant. Although the whole plant is potentially contained in the seed, it requires time to transform into the plant. It's the same way with all universes. God is sitting within each soul, and the soul has to become aware of it. The degree of awareness is known as Self-Realisation or God-Realisation. In all these universes, the whole eternity can be contained in the eye of a sparrow.

Take a close look at this seed. At present, do you see the marigold plant inside? The answer is no.

Inexperienced Seed or Soul

Now, if we put this seed in soil and water the soil to provide some moisture, in a few days it will help the seed to open up. Soon it will appear out of the soil not as seed but as a small plant. With time, it will grow in size and know its existence as Self-Realisation. Later, its roots will become stronger and steadfast in soil. With the help of good weather (a teacher), it will produce very admirable flowers. Everyone loves its fragrance and admires its beauty.

Realisation of self as Soul

God-Realisation giving fragrance to others

Now, if we keep this seed for one hour in soil and twenty-three hours in outside weather, will this seed grow? The answer is no. We can keep this seed in this condition for the next forty years, and it will never grow. It is same with our spiritual unfoldment. Stay within the moisture of Spirit, and you will see the results. You do not have to tell others what you do; your fragrance will pull them towards you. This small example is good enough if you want to grasp my point.

Your sincere effort will never go wasted.

SON OF GOD

This is one of the most famous lines in Christianity: Jesus Christ is known as the Son of God. That is true, but it does not mean he is the only Son of God in this world. Every soul created by God has the right to claim this title, but this title has to be earned. Jesus was known to be the Son, but again, up to what extent was he successful in his effort? No one knows.

What is the Son of God? Any person or soul who can earn good karma and hold similar qualities to God is the Son of God. It is very difficult for even the majority of known saints to fail on this point. It is almost the same as God operates in this world. Now the question is, can you operate your life on this basis? Maybe a few times you can maintain this state of consciousness, but to maintain it for a day or forever is not possible.

Even if an iota of five passions is present in your thoughts, you will fail. Now you see what the requirements are to claim this title. If you study the history of saints at present or in the past, you will find there is some evidence of one or more of the five passions. My experience in this field shows only the direct representatives are able to claim this quality, but at times even they fail to maintain this state of consciousness at this level. Now you see how difficult it is to maintain this title.

God's qualities are infinite. Here are just a few.

Universal

Any Son of God must have a universal thought or approach to all life forms. To kill another of God's creation is a big sin. Jesus was helping his followers to catch fish in the sea and then eat them as food or to sell for the same purpose. Any religious guru who does this is not a Son of God in my vocabulary. It is not Jesus alone; the majority of the world saints fail on this point. In effect, Jesus Christ himself said, "I am the Son of man." Later, Christians changed it into Son of God.

Freewill

Most of the saints fail on this point as well. They recommend their followers not leave their teachings, and they mention a number of consequences that will happen if they do leave. Instead of teaching them universal thought and saying farewell, they build fear in their minds. So, any saint who is attached to any religion cannot hold universal thought. Being religious means, you are for or against other systems.

Omnipotence, Omniscience, Omnipresence

This means: All powerful, all knowing and all presence. Can any saint hold this state of consciousness? Not a single saint, because they come for a number of years to spread the message of God in their own ways. Then at the end of their physical life spans, their future spiritual journeys are untraceable.

Creator

God created everything—souls and the universes. Is there any saint in our written history who can create souls? I know what they can do, and many of them are responsible for creating or being part of religious wars. They were responsible for killing uncountable human lives. That leads to suffering of their families and millions of negative karmas created. Can these saints be called the Sons of God?

Giver

God is responsible for the whole creation and also provides food and shelter without anything in return. Can any saint do this? The answer is no. Instead of giving, they are always asking for donations. These donations are used to run their cult systems. God runs the whole world but never asks for any donation. They are so stubborn that instead of saying thanks, the majority of them don't even believe that God exists.

It never complains or punishes; instead, it has given us free will to believe or not believe. It makes no difference to God. If in life we do a small favour to our friends or family members, and if we do not hear a thank-you, within a reasonable time it upsets us. Do we have God qualities? The answer is no.

Tolerance

It is a known factor that if others are not in tune with us, we are not agreeable to tolerate their presence. There are extremist believers in religions, but they're not direct believers in God; to them, their religious leader or saint is God. There are many who swear at God because they know God does not punish them. As the universal creator, it does not discriminate between believers and non-believers. Can any saint do this? As I said earlier, we all are children of God as souls.

But to give the title "Son of God" to any physical or human is not justifiable. As I said, the words *physical* and *human* indicates it is not possible to be the Son of God because God is formless, and we can never be so. Or if we are formless, then we will never be known in this world as saint; we will never be heard of. All the lower worlds are schooling for souls, and we are learning to live in its presence. All souls are equal, and the only difference is in our states of consciousness.

One day we will have awareness of God and feel its presence invested within us as souls. Any saint or religion claiming "I am the only way" is totally untrue. This statement indicates it is not a universal thought and does not allow your free will to choose what you want to follow or tolerate. The bigger the promises, restrictions, and followers, the bigger is the deception. God created each soul with the ability to find its own way to its creator.

For an example, a mother tortoise lays eggs at the beach and hides them under sand. When the eggs hatch after seventy days, their mother is not there to guide them, but they walk straight to water. During this journey, many of them are picked off by eagles or similar birds. In the physical plane, this is exactly what happens to us as well. Do not follow any pseudo-master. Any person who listens or follows the dictates of these people is very weak in nature and not yet ready to be directly in the presence of God. You are an individual, and with your efforts, one day you can be the Son of God.

SPIRITUAL TRAVEL

Practice 1

As you are sitting, take a very close look at the ceiling and pattern of plaster, or the shadows of light. At home, you can put some kind of **cross** on the ceiling, permanently where you practice daily. Once you have visualised, close your eyes and relax by taking a few deep breaths. Put your attention on the third eye and visualise the ceiling. Now forget completely that you are sitting on the ground.

In your imagination, feel that you are near the ceiling; the distance between the ceiling and your eyes is only six inches, and you are looking at the pattern of plaster or the shadows. To make it more realistic, you can try to touch the ceiling with your hands. Repeat this a number of times if you're not successful on first attempt. Try again till you're successful.

Practice 2

This time, we repeat the same technique but from different angle. Take a very close look at the window area and visualise all things nearby. You can choose another location most suitable from your sitting position. Then close your eyes and relax by taking a few deep breaths. Again, put your attention on the third eye and visualise the window area as before, remembering all the details. This time you are not going to reach the window.

You will try to **be there** as soon as you possibly can. As you are standing near the window, try to look back at your physical body from the angle of window or your chosen spot. You can also try to run from your position to the window and then look back at yourself. You can look at others as well, if it makes you feel more realistic. This is called the Saguna-Sati (instant) technique. It can work two ways.

Either you are looking at yourself from the window area in the soul body, or I will not be surprised if your whole body moves near the window or chosen spot. If it happens this way, it is called direct projection— shifting your body to the desired place. The speed of action in this exercise is very important, and this is why I said run, not walk. Repeat this as many times as possible until successful.

May success be yours.

—

SPIRIT

Spirit is the essence of God. It is the life force for all its creation, and without it nothing can survive or exist. It is the bonding material for everything you can think of. Everything is created out of Spirit. Without Spirit, all universes will be unseen or non-existent; the whole space will appear as a big void, and no one will be there to witness it. The first creation out of Spirit is light and sound. Light provides the visibility, and sound becomes the bonding material.

Light is used as knowingness of God's presence, and sound is the communication between God and its creation. Pure light is so clear that everything is seen as non-existent, but eventually it appears as a very light shade of white and then pure white. After Anami-Lok, it begins to appear as a very light gold, and it's a pure gold colour in the soul plane. In the lower worlds, colours change dramatically, and in the physical plane it appears as a rainbow. Out of this rainbow, you can create millions of colours.

Pure sound is total silence, and out of this silence you hear the hum. In the soul plane, you hear the single note of a flute. In the lower worlds, sounds change according to the vibrations of each plane. In the physical world, it becomes the Sa Re Ga Ma Pa, Dha, Ni, Sa and out of this all world music is created. If you add all the sounds of this world, it will be heard as a hum. It's the same with colours: if you mix all the colours of rainbow, you will be surprised to see the result. It will appear as a pure white colour.

The whole colour theory of TV is based on this factor: it is RGB (red, green, blue), and a combination of these three is YMC (yellow, magenta, cyan). Add all these colours, and the result will be white. In the same way, everything is created out of Spirit, and we see the result in lower worlds, in materialistic forms such as land, mountains, sky, humans, and animals. As soon as we begin to leave the lower worlds, we begin to fade away. Humans cannot see if you appear to them in the astral form.

The soul plane is the last plane when you appear as a soul and almost look like a physical replica. After that, this identity begins to fade away in the misty worlds of Spirit. Eventually you will totally disappear as any kind of identity regarding what you look like at present. You will retain your individual identity as a assistant of God, but you disappear into this big, unseen void of God. The total experience is that everything is created out of Spirit, and it merges back into its creator.

Now you see that nothing can exist without Spirit. The balance of all planets, universes, and the total galaxy is held in place by Spirit. In the lower worlds, this pure Spirit becomes negative or positive, black or white magic, and many other examples. Going back to the colour theory, if we add RGB, the colour will be white, and the combination of RGB is YMC, which is also white. If we retain YMC, which is equal to white but minus red, green, and blue, the result will be black.

Now you see that you can also create black out of white as well. Spirit is unlimited and very similar to its creator, God. This is why all the saints, saviours, and prophets fail to know God fully: because you are its creation but not God. God is the creator, Spirit is our lifeline, and God breathes through us all to show its presence. Beingness is a state of pure Spirit, and this is why there are no limits in travelling. Spirit is everywhere, and so are you in a being state.

All the lords of higher planes live in a beingness state, and they are so close to God that they are almost pure Spirit as well. When saints in the lower worlds sit in meditation for longer period, such as a month, a year, or longer, they become channels for this Spirit. As the Spirit flows through their bodies, it nourishes the physical body for its well-being. Many ask, "How can this be possible?" My answer is, "Why don't you try?"

All shadows disappear in pure light, and so does all materiality in pure Spirit. All the pains or pleasures are part of negative Spirit, and spiritual freedom is part of pure Spirit. Humans are depending on materialistic security, and that is why we moan and groan. Despite all the food facilities, we are always short of food. Birds have no permanent homes, but they roam from branch to branch and are happy. The will of God is their security, all the food is provided, and they never go hungry.

We are the closest to God and have more means of exploring its worlds. We have the ability to achieve anything at our disposal. But we have lost our trust in Spirit because our prophets and priest-craft have failed to show us the true path. Our true security lies within. Spirit is the creator, and Spirit is the way. The day you become aware of this, you will know all. Until then, you will struggle as you have done all along.

The temple within is the house of Spirit, but due to your materialistic desires, you have rented it out to Kal, the negative Spirit within. Your desires will never end, and that is the main cause of human suffering. These desires create a big void between yourself and Spirit. You are so close to God, and it is so close to you via Spirit. It is through this Spirit that you can communicate with the spiritual Master. It is through this Spirit that the spiritual Master shows his presence to all his Seekers.

Those who recite too many verses are depending on religious words but not on God. They will never experience the pure Spirit until they change their practice in believing. External is the reflection of inner, and external is negative or positive, whereas inner is pure Spirit. The end of life should be celebrated with a laugh. You can only laugh if you can fly away with five elements as pure Spirit. Now we know God is everywhere as Spirit, and any Seeker, when in meditation, becomes the centre of universe.

At that time, there is no holier place than where you are sitting. Only mortals travel from one temple to another when they can be viewed instantly. Live Spirit is the true temple. The other temples are mind pleasing only. Spirit is pure essence of God, and this is why it is the life force for all God's creation and is found in every flower of earth—and you as well.

Spirit is always with you.

SPIRITUAL CHAKRAS

Indian saints were the first ones to explore spiritual chakras, so all the credit goes to them. On this subject, I am only going to write very briefly because we do not practice these chakras, and because you can find lots of information on the internet or provided by many yoga groups.

Muladhara Chakra: It is the four-petalled lotus centred at the rectum, and the colour is red. It is the seat of the earth element and the first stage of the yogis. The word to be used here is Kaling.

Kundalini: It is a pair of snakes lying wrapped or coiled in sleep, waiting for the right concentration to arouse them for Ridhi-Sidhi powers. It centres between the Muladhara and Swadhishthan chakras.

Swadhishthan Chakra: It is focused at the reproductive organs and represents the creative powers. The colour is orange and is a six-petal lotus. It is the water element and the second stage of yoga. The word repeated here is Onkar.

Manipurak Chakra: It is the eight-petal lotus. The colour is yellow, and it is the seat of the fire element. It is located opposite the navel in the spinal cord, and it represents the sustaining and nourishing power. The Manipurak chakra is the third state in the practice of yoga, and the word repeated is Hiring.

Anahag Chakra: It is the twelve-petal lotus. The colour is green. The Anahag chakra is focused on the heart centre and represents the destructive power. It is also the breath centre and the seat of the air element. The word to be used here is Sohang.

Vishudha Chakra: It is the sixteen-petal lotus. It is concentrated at the throat and is the seat of the ether element. The colour here is blue, and the word the yogis use for repetition is Shring or Ashtang.

Do-dal Chakra: It is the two-petal lotus and is indigo in colour. It is located behind the two eyes and is the sixth stage of the yogis. Do-dal is ruled by the mind element and is opened by a repetition of the word Aum. It is also known as the pituitary gland or the seat of the mind.

Third-Eye Chakra: This is the true chakra, known as the seat of the soul. This is where Spirit enters through the crown chakra to be in contact with the pineal gland and reach all lower chakras. The word to be used here is Haiome.

Crown Chakra: It is like a way station to have any success. Without this centre, Spirit cannot entre in to the body or any lower spiritual centres. It is known by many names: "soft spot" or "narrow is the way". It is very similar to a bottleneck, and a bottle can be filled or emptied through this opening.

Medulla Oblongata: It is situated very close to the pineal gland. It is at the beginning but rear point of your spine. This is another spiritual centre to do soul travel. This time the attention is focused mostly on the back wall or three to four feet behind you. You can use any spiritual word for practice.

When your outer world has been closed, and your inner world of thoughts and attention is fixed unwaveringly at the third eye, then you are ready to step across the invisible veil between the objective and subjective worlds. You should lose all feeling and sensation of the existence of the body.

SPIRITUAL LIFE

During one of our meetings, I was advising everyone to work hard and spend as much time as they possibly could to achieve their goals. A newcomer asked, "How would you sum up the whole lecture in one sentence?" My answer was, "To live your life as directed by God." These eight words can be your life changer, but otherwise we can write another holy book to explain it fully and in detail. Now, the question is are you living your life as directed by God?

There are thousands of religions in this world, and they have billions of followers. Out of these billions, probably only a few thousand people are following their lives as directed by God. Others are following the dictates of their religious systems, which are misleading in hundreds of ways. The majority of them are leading lives as directed by the mind, not God. They are so occupied in the turmoil of mind games that they fail to differentiate what is religious and what is spiritual.

Do you know all religious followers believe that they are living the life as directed by God, but they are not? All holy books are expressing the truth experienced by the prophets. Because these prophets are no longer living, their teachings are turned into religion. Religion is a system to follow, and at the head are priest-craft. Any priest can read the holy book and claim to be the knower of what had been written in any religious book, but he is not the knower of **truth** as experienced first-hand by the prophets.

Priests are not saints; it is an adopted occupation to earn a living. Behind this occupation, lots of deception is carried on to mislead followers. This is done purposely to keep their jobs. Now, if this person is leading a life of deception himself, how could he guide you to live your life as directed by God? They use all the tactics to create funds, and some religions recommend their followers donate 10 percent of their hard-earned money without fail. God does not want any money, so who does?

Some of the funds are spent on buildings known as temples. Is God living in these buildings? God is living within each soul, known as the essence of God's Spirit, which can be experienced at any time because we have been bestowed with the power of creativity. Most of the funds are used to build temples and pay the salaries of people working in the system. The rest is used against other religions to create holy wars. Many countries have been destroyed, and millions have lost their lives.

Due to this, their spiritual experiences are at halt. Now, who is responsible for this? They are our religious leaders, and these people with devious minds have hatred for other religions. Are they going to teach you how to live your life as directed by God? They all are lost individuals in their lives in many ways—otherwise, they would not be living at the expense of others. If you become an extreme follower of any religion, you are a failure in the eyes of God because you have become for or against other religions or other souls.

By doing this, you have moved at least one step away from the workings of God because you have created a wall between himself and the rest of the creation of God. Now, will God accept you as its near or dear one? Ask this question to yourself. It does not matter what you follow to know God's ways; you must hold a universal approach to the rest of God's creation, and that is to love all its creation as you love God. None of the religions at present hold this universal approach.

Christians provide door-to-door service on Sunday to increase their following. Islam believes in conversion of this world into one religion.

They have one good approach to believe in Allah only, not to worship any idealism of prophets or statue. That is a direct approach to God, but other than this, their approach towards this world is not on neutral grounds. Many holy wars are being fought, known as jihad. We cannot expect the whole world to become one.

God has created each soul individually to gain spiritual experience in its own way. Free will is the key to spiritual success. God does not interfere in our right or wrong actions; the mistakes we make are taken as our experiences in life. Then who are these religions and their priest-craft to dictate the lives of their followers? They all are against the individual thought of living. Those who don't follow are known as non-believers or Kafir. I love this word *Kafir*. Do you know why? Because the whole world is full of Kafirs.

It does not matter what religion you follow; it applies to every religious person in this world because no one approaches God directly. All religious followers are only interested in the intermediators, known as prophets or gurus. They all fail to see the mirror. When you see yourself in the mirror, only then does the reflection of your true look let you see what you look like. Otherwise, everyone believes that he or she is pretty. Ninety-nine percent of the population of this world is in deception of true believing.

Only God can decide whether you are following his ways. All religions say, "Our holy book is holding a higher truth than other religious books. Our customs and costumes are better than others. Our prophet is the only one who have been closer to God or sent directly by God." Many mythological stories are created to prove that it is the only truth. He is the Son of God. We all are souls of God, created individually to experience in the lower worlds and face the five passions of mind, controlled by the negative force.

One day we may become the assistants in good cause in God's worlds. All these religions and their followers are under the dictates of Kal and are misled in believing that whatever they are doing is the will of God, when it is nothing more than the dictates of negative power in action. I wish we all stand clear from our religious beliefs and view ourselves on a neutral basis to know the truth. I talk to many people this way, and the usual remarks are, "We are never taught this way," but it does make sense to all open-minded people.

Now at least they know, and one day they apply this principle in life, face reality, and are one step closer to God. Before, they were miles away from God, although at times they felt they were close to God and were doing God's work, not knowing their approach was opposite to what God expected of them. Half of the animal kingdom is created in a way to kill or be killed by others in order to experience life. Half of the animal kingdom is based on vegetation living.

Humans have already gone through this experience, and with spiritual unfoldment they are one step closer to Godly living. This is the difference between the animal and human kingdoms. By now, we should be the caretakers of the animal kingdom to assist God as co-workers. Most religious leaders and followers are slaughtering the creation of God, yet they believe they are God-loving people and are doing lots of charity work, when true charity is totally forgotten.

"Live and let live" is the key to success. In all of creation, all living things have the right to live in this world as they wish. You may be surprised to learn that many religions don't believe that animals have souls; if you are one of them, that is why you are still part of the Kal team. Now, I'll give you some examples to prove that there is very little difference between yourself and the knowingness of animals. They have very similar feeling towards their children.

I was watching a nature programme on TV, as I do most of the time. I believe there are many facts of life we can learn from them. There was a herd of elephants, maybe about thirty in number. I noticed most of their calves were walking in the middle of the grown-ups. The young ones were protected, and they walked many miles towards their destination during the drought season to find water. During their journey, one of the calves fell sick due to lack of water and milk from the mother as nourishment.

Because the mother was very weak and starving herself. The baby began to crumble, and the rest of the herd kept moving, but the mother of this calf stayed put with her child. As they were left behind alone, hyenas and lionesses circled around to hunt. The mother protected her child all through this ordeal and kept watch over her child, sensing the poor health condition. She saw and felt the last breath of her child, and once she was sure that her child was no more, only then did she move on to find her herd.

During this whole experience, I felt that the animals understand the value of life more than we humans do. Now, you call them animals and say that they have no soul? I am grateful to the Discovery Channel and to the team of people who brought this experience to the screen for us to learn something. There are millions of farmers throughout this world, and it is their business to raise animals for slaughter and then supply chains of stores.

Yet they all go to church on Sunday, and some go on Friday to ask for forgiveness. Who are they deceiving, God or themselves? For sure their actions are not directed by God. There are many religious days to be celebrated by the killing of animals, known as Bali, which means sacrifice. Eid is celebrated in Islam and involves a sacrifice of animals. Sacrifice to Kali-Mata in Hinduism and many tribes in the African continent.

The followers of Sikhism believe that they can eat meat because their last guru ate meat during his struggle with the Mughal Empire. Probably it was a need due to the circumstances they were living under. I don't argue with these people because they will find another excuse to win the argument. Then I go one step further. Can you name any of the gurus who drank alcohol? All ten gurus lived very ethical lives and set hundreds of examples for how to live our lives as directed by God.

Not a single guru drank alcohol, so why do their followers drink it? They are all misled people—not by the gurus or their religious book but by the priest-craft who are living similar lifestyles. Looking into facts and figures at present, we should not expect any pity from this world regarding the animal kingdom because they don't even spare the human kingdom. The war between Sikhs and Muslims started some four hundred years ago, and hundreds of thousands of people lost their lives on both sides.

It is sad to know people are still losing their lives every day at the India-Pakistan border. It is power, and hatred is responsible for this in the name of religion. Young and innocent boys are brain-washed and fully prepared to become suicide bombers. Yet every Muslim goes to Masjid on Friday and prays to Allah. I am not pinpointing Muslims; this is the routine practice of most religions. Hindus are no less in many ways.

Once India was known as the most religious place on earth, people visited here to experience religious or Godly feelings. At present, it is full of negativity, crime, rapes, greed, power, and many others. Those who don't believe in God are called atheists, but in many ways, they are better than religious followers, and I believe they are more-close to God because they can avoid many wrong followings. If we study most of the religions, we can probably find there is no fault in their prophets or holy books.

but in the followers failing to follow how to live their lives as directed by God. There are very few, who are the lovers of God, whereas others are God fearing, knowing their weaknesses and wrong-doings. They only follow religion to believe that by doing this, they are protected from their wrong-doings. This is why you will notice they only go to church or temple to ask or pray for forgiveness. My answer to this is:

Why do you have to ask for forgiveness and stand in shame in front of your creator? You should not be doing any wrong act in the first place.

God provides many opportunities in our lives, and for any one of them, we can make our turning point. God is forgiving as we forgive our children. Analyse all your actions in the future and ask, "Are these God-directed or mind-directed actions?" The answer is always within us. After some time, practice becomes a habit of no wrong-doing. Now, all your actions are directed by God, and you can lead the others to do the same. This world can be similar to heaven if we allow it to happen.

Now you are living your life as directed by God.

SPIRITUAL SIGNIFICANCE OF NO: 5

All known saints of this world have used the number five as a main number because it represents God in so many ways. Most of creation is based on this number.

Sach-Khand: The soul plane is the fifth plane from this physical world. The planes are physical, astral, causal, mental, and soul plane.

Humans: When this world was ready for human occupation, God sent the first five people to this earth. This is also mentioned in Hinduism (Puran-Granth) as the five Raj kumars.

Humans have five bodies altogether to use one on each plane to attain Jivan-Mukty.

Human body have five main parts: head, two arms, and two legs. You will notice most of the animals and birds have six main parts; this is the reason they cannot achieve Jivan-Mukty in this life when humans can.

Animals have a head, a tail, and four legs.

Birds have a head, a tail, two wings, and two legs.

Humans depend on the number five. We have five fingers on each hand and each foot.

Humans are created with five elements: Spirit, water, fire, air, and earth.

Human life is controlled by five passions: Kam, Krodh, Lobh, Moha, and Ahankar.

Humans have five senses to experience this world: taste, touch, smell, sight, and hearing.

Humans need five virtues to attain Jivan-Mukty: wisdom, love, truth, goodness, and justice.

Humans have five tastes: sweet, sour, bitter, pungent, and salty.

This world is created with five continents: Europe, Asia, Africa, Oceania, and America.

The Olympics has five rings to represent each continent.

This world has five oceans: Pacific, Atlantic, Indian, Southern, and Arctic.

God created five races of people: white, black, brown, red, and yellow.

God created five life forms or kingdoms: humans, animals, birds, sea life, and the plant kingdom.

Canada has five great lakes: Erie, Huron, Michigan, Ontario, and Superior.

The Punjab has five rivers: Sutlej, Beas, Ravi, Chenab, and Jhelum.

China has five sacred mountains.

Sikhism

Guru Gobind Singh Ji created Sikhism. He chose five Pyare, or loved ones: Daya Singh, Mohkam Singh, Sahib Singh, Dharam Singh, and Himmat Singh.

There are five religious verses: Japji sahib, Jaap sahib, Tav Prasad swaiye, Chaupai, and Anand sahib.

He recited five bania (religious verses) to prepare Amrit (spiritual nectar).

He gave five times Chulle Amrit (handful) nectar to drink each Pyara.

He sprinkled five times Amrit in their eyes.

He sprinkled five times Amrit on their heads or hair.

He gave five kakkars: Kesh, Kangha, Kashhera, Karha, and Kirpan.

There are five virtues: Sat/truth, Daya/kindness, Santokh/contentment, Nimrata/humility, and Pyar/love.

There are five Takhats of Sikhism (seat of authority): Akal Takhat Amritsar, Damdama Sahib, Keshgarh Sahib, Hazur Sahib, and Patna Sahib.

There are five bowels in each line of Gurumukhi. (Language alphabet)

In a Sikh wedding and engagement, there are five rituals with five fruits used five times.

Islam:

They pray five times daily.

There are five pillars of Islam: faith, prayer, charity, fasting, and pilgrimage to Makkah.

They have used the number five three times in the Qur'an.

Jewish

The Torah contains five books.

There are five books of Moses.

Christianity

There were five wounds on Christ.

The number five is used 253 times in Bible.

Buddhism: They have five commandments.

You will not kill or harm living things.

You will not steal

You will not have wrong relationships.

You will not tell lies or speak unkindly.

You will not drink alcohol or take drugs.

Jainism: They have five bows.

Ahimsa: non-violence

Satya: truthfulness

Asetya: receive no free lunch or gifts

Brahmacharya: No adultery

Aparigraha: avoid excessive attachment

They have five colours in their flag: white, red, orange, green, and dark blue.

They have five supreme beings: Arhats, Siddhas, Acharyas, Upadhyayes, and Sadhu.

Hinduism

They use five items during a wedding ceremony: flower, coin, durva grass, turmeric, and rice.

Naag panchami is the worship of snakes on **5** Sawan (July/August) every year.

Generally

As you have noticed, the number five has been used by all religions.

"High five" is a sign of agreement.

A star has five points.

A starfish has five arms.

The number five is considered as a sign of freedom.

The five-pointed star represents the planet Mars (Mangal), which is considered lucky.

Five is the first digit to form a circle.

TO BE OR NOT TO BE

The title of this section was written by William Shakespeare in *Hamlet*. It is well said and applicable to all spiritual Seekers. It is time to make a decision. Do you know the majority of population cannot decide from birth till death, "What they want to do in life? They follow the family pattern of living, and they feel successful. You need to walk out of this system, decide as an individual soul, and set a goal for yourself. This goal should be something of an outstanding nature.

Nearer the time of leaving this world, you should be able to say, "Yes, I have done something I wanted to do, and I am successful." I set up my goal at a very early age, and I am successful, yet I feel I could have done a lot more if some-how I had a better platform to stand on or work from. After all my success, I still have to face the negativity thrown by others, which is expected as long as we are living in this world.

My advantage is that at least I can understand and bypass many situations with the help of Spirit. I notice one of the main problems of a spiritual Seeker is age and responsibility. Everyone wants to experience God in this life, but people are not really interested in God. They are seeking quick solutions, if some-how they can perform miracles. This is to satisfy their own minds and tell others how extraordinary they are.

It is all illusion thinking because it is not going to work that way or that quickly. To do these things, you have to lay a very strong spiritual foundation. If your spiritual foundation is strong, then you don't have to create miracles to impress others. Miracles will happen in their own accord. I purposely do not create any miracles, but Spirit is creating many miracles on my behalf. People come and tell me how and what they have seen.

It is nothing of my own doing; this point was cleared long ago by Jesus Christ upon asking about many miracles. He replied, and of my own I do nothing. It is the Father who does all, and he said something in this manner. I don't think any true saint purposely tries to create miracles to impress the followers. If you do, there will be some price to be paid by going through some kind of sufferings. Only magicians create illusive magic to earn their living.

All young followers have one thing in mind: that I am still young. What is the big rush to become a serious spiritual Seeker? Although they are still following, they find many avenues on the side. Some are good, and many can derail them. Time goes on, and these other avenues multiply. Some are part of increased responsibility with age, and many cling on to our wrong-doings. There is always some nudge from the Spirit, but you are unable to shake them off.

Some have become a part of you until your last breath in this world. The question remains the same: "To be or Not to be." You wanted to **be** something or someone, but are you able to add another four letters with it—**come**? To execute your dream, you have to **become** what you wanted to be originally. We keep repeating these few words, but we never had the ability to execute them. We are so tangled up in life that we always fail to find time.

These few words are applied in all fields; either it is spiritual, business, or politics. We set our goal and begin to work around as required. With business, in time you can see some growth, and that will build up self-confidence. Business can be done with honesty, and it may be with slow growth, but there are no restrictions that you cannot do any wrong. You can have lots of negative traits and still be successful. Politics is the same.

Although you have gained qualifications accordingly, it may not be required, but you carry lots of negative or deceptive traits to succeed; otherwise, it will not be called politics. Do you know it is much easier to become prime minister of any country than become a true saint? A saint is a symbol of purity. It is lots of hard endeavours and very slow progress. Any proper saint will never have the courage to declare that he is spiritual because he knows that there is much more to know and achieve.

The more he achieves, the more-humble he becomes, and he declares to people that he is no higher than anyone. It is people around him who experience the difference and praise his state of consciousness. It is very hard to find a true saint in this Stone Age, although at least one million people are claiming to be saints. Most of them are fake or pseudo-masters; they all are after making money. Do you know that if you want to make quick and easy money, you should claim yourself to be a saint?

You don't have to do anything; people will come in flocks with cash. Although they all want to make money, it is their belief that you will help them to make quick money. At present, there are a number of very famous saints in India who are behind bars for their wrong-doings. They were all criminals and were running criminal activities with the help of politicians, boosted by their followers, who are poor and were looking for a shoulder to lean on.

These criminal-minded people take advantage of your weaknesses. Now they are serving long terms behind bars, charged with murder, rape, robbery, abduction, money laundering, and more. Now, why did we mention these people in this chapter? Because they were claiming to be saints and failed to become saints. These are the people who give a bad name to spiritualism, and people lose faith in God.

The original question is still here: To be or Not to be? It is very hard to make a decision in life and execute your decision. Jesus Christ also mentioned wolves disguised as sheep. It is very difficult to judge because of their appearance, which represents them to look like saints. Spiritual Seekers must make up their minds. Lead your life because we all have to live in this world, but priority must be given to our set goal—that is, to experience God in this lifetime.

I heard someone say something to the effect, "Yes, I am sure. I will be more serious in later years." I wish it could work out that way. With age, we have more responsibilities, worries, and ill health. Even if you try to fulfil your goals, I am sure you will face lots of disappointments. We have been dreaming about our set goal but have failed to execute it.

To make a core decision in life is one of the most difficult. For those who do decide, God does not fail them. The obstacles will be many, but nothing can stop those who want to dwell in the ocean of love and mercy. To be is a question, but to become is your decision. Once you do become with full realisation, then you learn that you only wanted to be similar to your creator God. Be yourself and let the others be.

You will dwell in the heart of God.

—

VICTIMS OF THE CIRCUMSTANCES

Many famous people have been victims of the circumstances, such as Jesus Christ, Sri Guru Arjan dev of Sikhism, and others. When you are a victim of the circumstances, and that completely changes the destiny of your life. Your suffering is inevitable and beyond your control, and life is wasted because of this. Will you ever be able to turn the clock back? May the Spirit be with you. Guru Arjan dev took the circumstances created by Muslims as the will of God.

Later, gurus stood up against these circumstances, and out of these circumstances a new religion formed from Hinduism, known as Sikhism. There are so many wars and civil wars going on within countries, a few power-hungry people or politicians create the situations, and the amount of destruction that takes place is beyond imagination. This will destroy tremendous amounts of property, which they are unable to replace for a number of years.

Human lives are lost, families are destroyed, and all these people who leave their countries and take refuge in safe countries become refugees. These people are victims of the circumstances. Sri Paul Ji was very successful in spreading the message of God, and some religions felt the threat. During one meeting in Spain, he was poisoned, and a year later he passed away. The circumstances of this spiritual path changed.

A new Master took over, and later he passed the spiritual word over to another Master.

Due to many reasons, they could not get along, and within this organisation circumstances changed. This organisation split into two paths, and so did the followers. Many are still confused even today and ask, "How can it happen on this pure spiritual path?" I was destined to be the future of some organisation, but I have been the victim of circumstances due to this and a few other times as well. There is a saying: if two birds are tied together, although they have four wings, they cannot fly.

I feel the opposite. I am free as anything, but I always feel that my wings have been clipped. This means I can make the effort to fly, but I never will. That is the reason that despite having a higher state of spiritual consciousness, I failed to be recognised by many people as a saint. When looking at my failure, I take it as the will of God, but at the same time I know it is not true. Many people come to me crying for help, and their stories are very painful.

I tell them to create good karma so that their lives can be improved. Some are responsible for their self-created circumstances, and many are the victims of the circumstances created by their own friends or families. I know well-educated people, well-defined body builders, and so many other able people unable to succeed because they are under the shadow of others who are more influent. These people become the victims of the circumstances.

Mrs Hillary Clinton is very intelligent and is capable of becoming the president of America. First, she was the wife of Bill Clinton, and once he made a statement that his wife helped him to be a better president. Then she helped Mr Barack Obama for number of years. In 2016, she tried again to fight the presidential election against Mr Donald Trump.

She was more intelligent than Mr Trump but was not accepted as the first female president; she lost the election in November 2016. She became the victim of the circumstances, and I don't think she will try again because by the next election she will be too old. It does not matter how, but we all are victims of certain circumstances.

During the early eighties, the Indian government played its political game and placed one of their person "Pawn" in Punjab, so that Congress party could have a stronghold in that area. This person was very religious, and once he realised what the truth was, he backfired at the government. That led to the destruction of the Golden Temple in Amritsar and was followed by the assassination of the prime minister of India, Mrs Indira Gandhi.

Once the news spread that Mrs Indira Gandhi was no more, her body was kept for three days so that people could pay respects to her, but at the same time this party ordered their followers to carry out the massacre of Sikhs in Delhi. This also carried on for three days. I arrived in India on 28 October 1984 and she was assassinated on 31 October 1984 and I happen to be in Punjab and Delhi area that time.

The Government figures were very low but to my knowledge, well over ten thousand people were killed. Later more than sixty thousand youth lost their lives through fake encounters in Punjab. This only stopped when US President Bill Clinton intervened and made a very small statement to the effect "I think Sikhs are suffering in Punjab" then India Government got the message and everything stopped. All these people or families became victims of these political circumstances.

Up until today, these families are suffering, and no justice has been given. Those who persuaded Mrs Indira Gandhi to attack Golden Temple are still roaming free. I always sympathise with the victims of circumstances because the majority of them are innocent people. Their karmas are being mixed up with unknown people, and that was beyond their control. Now I will give you an example of who creates these circumstances.

India and Pakistan are firing on the border every day. If you watch the news on both sides, they are blaming each other. I know both sides are not saints. The political leaders are more interested in maintaining their status, and in order to do that, many people die. Do they care? I don't think so. It is the same story in a few Islamic states.

North Korea and America are doing the same. Nothing has happened yet, but they are on the verge of creating something similar. I will call these self-created circumstances, which will harm so many in the future.

—

VILLAIN OR SAINT

Ravana of Sri Lanka, Doryodhna of India, and so many others are the names of frustration. A saint can turn into a villain, and the biggest villain can turn into a saint. There are so many examples, such as Balmiki and Ashoka. When you are extremely negative or positive, that can become your turning point in life. Very wise person can turn into extremely foolish, and any foolish can turn into a wise man. Many people believe that I am successful physically and spiritually, but I have been through many failure points, and that could have turned me into a villain.

It was God and Satnam Ji who kept me in balance, and because of them, my clock kept ticking in the right direction. I can understand the frustration of others who have turned into villains. This is why my sympathy is always with them. I hope the clock can be turned back for them; then they could have lived very decent and honourable lives. Once you are tagged as a villain, you will be known as such forever. We will discuss the background of such people very briefly.

King Ravana is known as a very famous villain in Hinduism. Was he really a villain? Or has the Hindu religion believed it as such, and at present priest-craft talk about it all the time, only telling half the truth to their followers? No one takes the side of Ravana or talks about his goodness. Ravana was the most educated in religious studies, he was a great scholar of the vedas and worshipper of Lord Shiva. The foundation of the war between Sri Ram and Ravana was his sister, Shurpanakha.

She was the main character and cause of this war between them. She fell in love with Lakshmana, the younger brother of Sri Ram. Lakshmana got angry, and that was his character in life as an angry young man. He cut the nose of Shurpanakha, and she complained to her brother, King Ravana. Then the king got angry at this insult, and he planned something similar to teach them a lesson. He abducted Sita, the wife of Sri Ram.

Lakshmana could have told her politely that he was not interested. People often condemn Ravana, but his actions can be seen as a reaction to the mutilation of his sister's nose. War began. Who started it first, and who is the villain? To love someone is not a crime. There are ways of coming to some other conclusion. Sri Ram's father, King Dasharatha, was married to three women at the same time. It was the deceitful doings of Sri Ram's stepmother, Kaikeyi, and that was why they ended up in exile.

Again, the basis of this war was on Ram's side, and during this war many thousands lost their lives on both sides. If Sri Ram, Sita, and Lakshmana were not in exile, this situation would have never occurred. We often overlook and point a finger at others to make them look like villains, when the actual culprit is sitting right under our noses. Up until today, all Hindus burn the statue of Ravana every year on Dessehra day, and they celebrate the win on Diwali day.

"Was Ravana really a villain? Who was responsible for making him one? Although Ravana was a highly religious person, sometimes it is very difficult to control or balance the flow of Spirit, which can turn into anger. Sri Ram was also a victim of circumstances first created by his stepmother. Second, the anger of his brother Lakshmana led to a big war. King Dasharatha, the father of Ram, also died at the shock of Ram's exile for twelve years.

The root cause of destruction was Kaikeyi, not Ravana as believed. Ravana and all others were the victims of circumstances. Did you ever notice that true villains often walk away from the situation, and innocent ones are trapped to suffer for generations? I was and still am a victim of the circumstances, and I cannot talk about it openly. "Do you know why? Because it is all backfiring on me, the totally innocent party. Now, what can you do about it? Nothing.

There are so many fake villains known as pseudo-masters and pretending to be saints, but their motive is to gather money and make a chain of properties—and they have no shame of doing this. These people commit extreme acts and end up behind bars. In the modern era, there are so many saints in prison—for example, Baba Asa Ram and Baba Ram Rahim, Rampal, and so many others in India. They had millions of followers visiting them every year, and in the eyes of their followers they were Gods.

But in return they abused their trust, and people lost their faith in these "Masters" and walked away from religion and their belief in God. Their assets are in the millions of US dollars. If truly you are a saint, you cannot even imagine how much advantage people take of you as well, because you have a goal to reach. You are humble, and in the majority of cases, Spirit doesn't help either. You are doing your best, but no one is protecting your back.

The insults you receive are unbearable and leave scars on your life forever. Anything can trigger you to be a villain. Then there are bandits who take full advantage of your weakness and rob you of everything. If you have any pride or goodness left in you, they will shatter it into pieces, and there is nothing you can do about it. Again, there is no back-up from Spirit. You can do nothing except hope one day you will succeed in your mission and everything will be OK.

When you can't reach the goal, the grapes are sour, as the saying goes; failure is at your doorstep. There are so many who will hold grudges and anger against you; that could be the result of your success or your decency, which they cannot tolerate. They could be normal or good people, but their own failures push them to become villains because they have nothing else to do. When you know your sufferings are caused by these people, it stirs anger within every moment to turn you into a villain and take revenge.

There is always something going within to stop you from taking any such action. Although you suffer, still Big Brother is not watching your back. Many times, I wondered why, and what I was getting by being or acting as a saint. I suffered all my life, but still I have not received any decent or solid answer. Many times, I ask, "Is all this really worth it?" At present I am not satisfied with my achievements. I suffered extremely, and villains are still roaming happily.

Who will justify this suffering and punish the culprits? As you can see, no justice has been done. We believe in karma, but if karma is not served in your lifetime, it may take place when you are not around. Then it has no value, and disappointments are many. I wonder sometimes is it really worth becoming a saint in the future? I may decline any such assignment in the future life unless it is agreed upfront. Many times, you ponder upon it and become a villain as well.

Now we take another example: who *did* become a villain in the eyes of his own people, although fighting for his throne, which was supposed to be rightfully his in the first place? This is the story of Mahabharata, another Hinduism war. It is regarding the throne of Hastinapur, UP, India, in approximately 3139 BC. There were three brothers: Dhritarashtra, Pandu, and Vidura (a half-brother). The eldest, Dhritarashtra, was born blind, and so the throne was passed over to second in line, Pandu.

Although Dhritarashtra was not happy about this situation, he could do nothing. Pandu should have been made the caretaker only until the son of the blind king grew up to an adult age. King Pandu was in the jungle and died at a very early age, and his five sons were young at that time. The throne of Hastinapur came back to Dhritarashtra (blind king) again. Dhritarashtra's eldest son, Duryodhana, became the rightful prince and heir to the throne, and he began to take responsibility.

At the same time, Pandu's sons were also grown-up, and they began to claim back throne, which at one time was their father's, with the help of Lord Krishna. Krishna played all the tricks in the book and misguided Duryodhana a number of times—for example, saying to not go naked in front of his mother, otherwise not even a hundred pandavas could kill him. The story is if he went naked at midnight in front of his mother, Gandhari, who had Siddhy (psychic) power, then he would receive a boon for protection and live forever.

That was part of the spiritual ritual. Krishna was directly responsible for the defeat and death of Duryodhana and many others I could name, but this is not the main discussion. The question is, "Was Duryodhana a villain?" I don't think so. There are certain rules in royal families that have to be followed. There is a law in England that any future king cannot marry any divorcee; if that is the case, then his throne will be passed over to another deserving member in the royal family.

At present, Prince Charles is to be the future king, but because he is married to a divorcee, it is possible that the British throne will directly be passed over to his son, Prince William from Queen Elizabeth II, unless they make changes in the law. The same thing happened in 1936 when King Edward VIII married an American, Mrs Wallis Simpson, who was already divorcee. He did not want to leave her, and so he abdicated himself to France.

The throne was passed to the present queen's father, King George VI. Otherwise, the history of the present royals would have been different. This example is related to Mahabharata's story. Blind King Dhritarashtra and Prince Charles are in the same situation, and so are

Prince Duryodhana and Prince William. At present, the British throne will not be passed over to the queen's second son, Prince Andrew.

Our present Queen Elizabeth II, whom I respect very much because she lived all her life ethically and did her duty with full responsibility, has gone through rough patches in her life due to her father, who died young, and difficulties in the marriages of her children. She is the mother of four children, and three are divorcees. It is such a trauma in life, being so powerful yet being unable to do anything about it. She has been the victim of circumstances.

Do you know during all wars, millions of people (we call them soldiers) die while fighting to achieve justice, and probably for only one person? Or are these all political games? All these soldiers are stuck in a catch-22. They have to follow the instructions without questioning, but once they die, their families suffer, and no one wipes their tears. Do you know they were the main breadwinners of their families? They were not villains but made to fight like villains.

Whoever kills another is not a saint; it does not matter what the cause is. Krishna said, or it is the belief of Hinduism, that he comes in every age to establish righteousness when things go out of control, karma-wise. These are all mythological stories, and there is more mythology in Hinduism than religion. There are so many self-created images of Gods which never existed in the way they portray them. Where was he during the world war1 and world war 2 when millions of people lost their lives?

Why did he not come to kill Adolf Hitler and so many other dictators? And there are so many living dictators at present. You will notice the majority of the followers are always naive and take these kinds of statements as their bible without question. If you do question, the priest will tell you another hundred stories to make it look like the whole truth. By having a wrong belief or following with blind faith, then you are the villain to yourself because you have closed the curtains to face the truth.

People believe that religions are important, but many don't know that all religions are man-made. All the extreme personalities come out of religions, which are dangerous to other religious practitioners and the general public. All suicide bombers come from some religion in this world. Now we look at another example. Ratnakar was a bandit from a very young age, and he murdered so many people before the age of thirty. Dramatic changes came in his life, and he decided to become a saint.

At present he is known as Balmiki, and he is the author of a religious book called the Ramayana. He looked after the wife of Sri Ram when Sita was separated from Sri Ram, and she gave birth to two sons, Luv and Kush. Balmiki was also the guru of Luv and Kush. Now you see a bandit or villain can also become a saint as well, and history is full of examples of such people. Ashoka was another one who was power hungry and killed so many people himself and with the help of his soldiers.

Once he saw so much blood, and then he realised he should lead a religious and ethical life. After thoroughly examining many religions, he decided to become Buddhist. According to ancient scriptures originally India was called "Jambudvipa" or "Indus" He changed it to "Bharat" and later it was changed to India. Now if we take the example of Ashoka and Ratnakar, this complete transformation can take place in one lifetime to any person, if destined to do so.

Do you know most of our previous famous prophets had been involved in wars, yet we still call them saints? As far as I am concerned, if any guru strikes another to kill, it does not matter what the circumstances are—at that time, he is not a saint. The followers are happy, but you cannot justify karmas committed. The person you killed was another soul, and God does not permit anyone to kill any of his creations. As they say, God is closer to you than your heartbeat or breath.

That is the difference between Villain and Saint. In Iraq, Mr Saddam Hussein was the villain to his people. Then super-villains came and killed him, and thousands of people died who were the victims of the circumstances. It is a belief in Sikhism that tenth Guru Gobind Singh and Aurangzeb use to meditate together in one of their previous lives. In their last historical lives, when they came face-to-face, Guru Gobind Singh acted as a saint, and Aurangzeb turned out to be a villain according to Sikhism and Hinduism history.

Something must have triggered Aurangzeb to commit such acts, or the family he was born in was responsible for his acts. Once you reach a certain crunch point, any villain or saint can transform into either character. If you can hold on to your nerve, then you are saint; if not, you become a villain. It is very sad that so many saints suffer at the hands of villains, and millions of people die every year without seeing or receiving any justice.

"Will there be one? People are scared for their lives and hiding, but culprits are roaming free and laughing. In English, there is a saying that every dog has his day. I know so many people who died but never had their day. This saddens me sometimes. I was given wrong advice by my own guru a number of times. I listened in good faith and followed instructions; due to that, I have suffered and am suffering today. Many times, I wonder why.

During my training into master-ship, I wished the floodgates of Spirit should open so I could pass the message of God. I noticed that I was fully controlled by the spiritual Master to not commit any mistake, but those who were doing wrong against me purposely were not. Now I have come to a certain age where I do wish no spiritual floodgates should open for me. God is the creator of the whole creation, and Kal is also part of God. With experience, I can say God is the creator and experiencer as well.

So, who is the Villain or Saint?

WEAK AURA & BLACK MAGIC

The majority of the time, we are responsible for our own suffering. Although we believe we are the followers of Spirit, at the same time we are following a number of other practices too. As the saying goes, you cannot sail in two boats at the same time. These other practices will become your failure point, and although you are trying to achieve something (extra knowledge), it provides resistance to the Holy Spirit, which brings so many difficulties to the Seeker of truth. Your spiritual aura becomes weak. In this weak aura many entities, black magic, or someone's anger can easily penetrate.

A. Take a look at this Golden ball which provides full Spiritual shield.

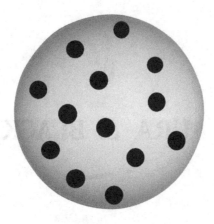

B. Now take a look at this Spiritual shield with lots of holes and provides less protection.

How to Remove This Entity

Once you become aware that someone else is also living within this aura, you will face lots of difficulties in life. It could be health or wealth problems, or this spirit can stir anger within you to create negative scenes in your family where everyone is disturbed by it. It's about time to take some action to remove this negative entity from your aura and lead your life back to normal. I will give you a very simple meditation exercise with a self-explanatory sketch.

Once you sit down in tailor fashion or any other acceptable position to meditate, take a few deep breaths to relax yourself. Repeat this breathing procedure until you feel fully relaxed. Begin to chant your holy word, or Haiome. Continue chanting until you feel the sensation of spiritual vibrations and a warm feeling within your forehead. When you are ready, create a spiritual circle or shield around yourself, as shown in the diagram.

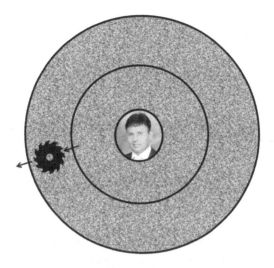

Next, create an image of a disturbing entity in your life. See in your vision that it is moving out of your spiritual shield or aura, as demonstrated during one of our practical workshops. Repeat this a number of times until you feel success.

May the success be yours.

~

DISCOVER YOURSELF

We have forgotten how to discover ourselves. We are more interested in discovery by someone else, but the biggest discovery is sitting within us. Guru Granth, the Bible, the Qur'an, the Gita, or any other is not your exploration of truth. You are abiding by someone else's explored truth. It is very common in Asian culture that if you want to leave your birth religion and find out what other religions or teachings are saying, it means there is something within, asking you to move on; there is more to learn.

This is only applicable to those who are true Seekers and want to explore spiritual truth for themselves. There is someone who knows better, and you are searching for this spiritual Master. We do this silently, or sometimes we declare openly, "I am off to follow this Master to more thoroughly find the truth." They will put all their effort into stopping you from doing this. They have many explanations for this. You should never follow a living Master; they are all misleading or will rob you off your money.

So, what do they recommend you do? Follow a book written by someone five thousand years ago. Can anyone tell me since when can a book be your living Master? You can believe what you like that is your freewill. They don't want you to leave their **circle**. It is their fear within that you may discover the truth. I have done my own exploration, and that is why I am writing something new every day. It is all coming from within. These people have gone rusty and can hardly think beyond their doorsteps.

Since I mentioned this word *circle*, I remembered my very own experience when I was child. This kind of life experience occurs quite often in village life. This is an example, and definitely I have no intention of ridiculing any person or religion. You may know female snakes produce at least one hundred eggs in one go. During my childhood, once I witnessed when they were hatching. The female snake formed a coil around all eggs during this process, and the baby snakes started to appear in no time.

There were so many, and some were making a desperate effort to get out of the coil due to a lack of space. Many made circles within the coil of the mother. To my surprise, the mother began to eat a number of them, and only few managed to escape; many lost their lives in this circle. To me, this was early learning and a turning point in my life. View this life with an open mind; you can learn an abundance of knowledge.

All these priests are not only concerned with their own followers, but they intervene into other religious followers as well. It is called forced religion conversion. This is the biggest sin anyone can commit. Those who accept conversion are from poor backgrounds, and all these priests take advantage of this and try to meet their physical needs, such as food and shelter. Unknowingly, these poor people walk into a trap.

When they do realise this conversion, the realisation comes that it was their own weakness, which was beyond their control. The agenda in their lives was to live; exploring within on a spiritual basis was totally unknown to them.

Michael was second in command "Manager" where I used to work, with at least four hundred people working under him. We were fairly close friends, and one day he came to see me for advice. He said, "Mr Gill, I am going to leave this job in a few days, can you advise me if I am making the right decision?" I asked why. He was under thirty years of age, and his future was ahead of him.

He said, "I want to explore this world, and I am arranging for a world tour." I advised him not to do it. I said, "You are so young and have such a highly paid and respectful job." "Well," he said, "I have made up my mind. This is the right time and age to explore this world. Later, I may not be able to do what I can do now." After a few days, he packed up his bags and explored the world to his maximum ability.

He had enough cash, but I asked, "If you run out of money, then what are you going to do?" He replied, "I don't mind washing dirty plates in some restaurant. This exploration is very important to me." That is what I call determination. How can this person fail in his life?

When I was so dedicated to discovering the truth, I had been ridiculed or insulted a number of times by my own near and dear ones, but I never cared. I did discover what I went out to discover, but at the same time those wounds of insults I received are still evident. This is why at present: I want to be alone and live in my self-explored world. All these relations we value most are nothing but pain to carry on our shoulders.

I discover something every day. Spirit asked me today to sit down and write. I took the whole dictation in twenty minutes on a piece of paper. I know all these things, but Spirit dictates me to write in such a manner, and I am amazed myself. Many people believe only in watching their own religious programmes on TV and not the others. They also recommend others not to watch other programmes.

In a sense, maybe they are correct, but at the same time it is their fear that you may discover something, which they don't want you to discover—the truth. I love all comedy programmes, and humour in life is very important. I used to watch *Father Ted*, and it was a Christian-based comedy programme. Father Ted was in the lead role, and Father

Dougal was a side role. Jack was the old father who always sat in his chair with a bottle (alcohol) in his hand.

It did not matter to him what subject was being discussed at any point of time—whenever they asked his opinion on what had been said, he always replied with one word: "Drink." That was part of the humour in this programme. Similar to Father Jack, a majority of the people have only one thing on their minds: drink, food, sex, or sleep. All these habits push you into the dungeons, and there are many ways to go in, but it's very difficult to come out.

The biggest truth is sitting within each individual, but these people will never let you set your own trap of discovery. I discovered many things while listening to many people from all walks of life. British mice live in the underground burrow system. You cannot catch mice by sitting outside the burrow. You have to put your hand in mice's den. It is possible that you may catch it, or the mice may bite your hand, but this is the only way to find the truth if mice do live in this burrow.

This is only an example—don't practice it. Truth comes to me every day, but quite often I fail to acknowledge it when I say I can remember it, or I don't bother to write it there and then. Ask yourself what have you explored so far. The answer will be almost nothing. The majority of people's exploration finish with eating spicy foods in some restaurant. You have only managed to explore part of the mind's faculty known as the Manas. In your whole life, your exploration comes to 0.1 percent.

My background is Sikhism, and once I was talking to another Sikh friend about God. I thought he was interested in knowing the truth, and so I offered him one of Sri Paul Ji's book to read. After a few days, he returned the book, and I asked him if he read it. He said yes. I said very good and left him there to ask further, if he was interested. After a short while, I learned through one of our common friends that he never read it because it was written by American white man.

He took it only to make fun of me. I never contacted him in the future. In his later years, he lived an alcoholic life and died from many organ failures, so he wasted his life doing nothing. He can never learn in his next hundred incarnations what I discovered in this life. Ignorance is the biggest obstacle in life, and he was so close to knowing the truth. I learned something while reading a book written by a red Indian saint and a few others.

All these people give you some idea of how to search for truth. If you imitate the life of some known saint, you can discover half the truth. When you discover the whole truth, then you also become a saint. Too much complaining about your life at present is the biggest obstacle to discovering any truth at all. All these Christians knocking on your door on Sunday are not there to show you the truth of God. They want you to join them. Truth is never discovered in groups; it is individual discovery.

It is never too late to discover yourself. Alexander the Great set his goal to conquer the whole world. Columbus was an Italian explorer and navigator who made four voyages and discovered America. New Zealander Edmund Hillary and the Sherpa Tenzing were the first two to climb Mount Everest. At the end of this chapter, you may ask yourself, "What did I discover?" You are right: nothing. Do you know why? Because you have never managed to set foot outside your doorstep.

Now, I have given a number of examples to discover yourself. I leave it in your hands. I cannot eat or drink on your behalf, and I can't discover things for you either.

My discovery is my own. You have to discover yourself.

DOOMSDAY OR DOOMED

The word *doomsday* is very frightening, and we expect something big to happen by nature in this world. That is true, but it does not happen quite often. Doomsday is a time of catastrophic destruction, where the world is going to end. Doomsday is a time of crisis, and on a small scale it takes place in everyone's life. Some are saying Kryptonians or a secret society of super-villains are going to come. Don't you think we already have a large number of super-villains in this world?

A fairly big doomsday is expected around 2030, but at present I am not certain of exact date of its happening. During the BC era, God instructed Noah to build an ark because heavy floods were coming to destroy that area. Recently, a tsunami came on 2 December 2004, hitting Thailand and nearby islands, and approximately 229,000 people lost their lives. These are natural disasters which don't happen quite often.

Within the last twenty years, we witnessed many wars and civil wars in Afghanistan, Iraq, Syria, and more. They all are man-created doomsdays, and people are suffering because of that. Nowadays, you cannot forecast which country is going to create a new doomsday for its own people or the rest of the world. At present, there are a few countries who are doomed by nature or by their group karma. Governments fail to provide water, food, or shelter to their citizens, and they are asking for help from well-off countries.

The person who is starving or hungry now is not going to wait for any doomsday—he is doomed now. Similarly, many of us are feeling doomed in our lives, not knowing why. We want to move on in our lives, but every time we fail due to many reasons, even though we are doing nothing wrong. It is our bad karma created somewhere which is holding us down, or it is some kind of psychic attack. Despite your good efforts and achievements, you cannot feel glorified.

You want to laugh, but there is little pain behind this, and so you cannot laugh openly. It is our doomsday which we have brought on us at some point in this life or in previous lives. We all admire our world, royal families, and any super-rich people because of their wealth and status. Do you know they are the most doomed people on earth because they have lost their free will? They cannot leave their palaces without taking a lot of precautions, and they cannot utter any rude words or make silly statements because they are answerable to every single word.

They cannot live normal lives and the palaces they live in. It is the biggest stage of acting, and you have to stay in character all the time. The Oscar awards are too small for their acting skills. It is their good karma to achieve all this limelight, and at the same time, it demands full payment in many ways. Any person from a middle-class family can lead a happier life than the royals. Royals and rich families are doomed to stay within the walls of big palaces, and they are the prisoners of being rich and famous.

Do you know that a good number of politicians are better actors than movie stars? It is their ability to deliver dialogues and command over language. It is the same with many known celebrities becoming rich and famous overnight, and it's equal to depression. Many become alcoholics or use heavy drugs. A name and fame can be lost in no time, and then they are forced to lead doomed, depressed lives which lead to suicides in many cases.

There are a number of natural doomsdays coming in the future, and at that time the power of Shiva the destroyer comes into action.

Now, I am going to give you some historical facts and figures about very famous people who created a doomsday for their own people and the rest of the world. All these people are responsible for the deaths of billions of civilians or military personnel during the last century to maintain their power.

Name	Ruled	Death Toll
Enver Pasha of Turkey	1913–18	1.1 million
Kim Sung of North Korea	1948–94	1.6 million
Ho Chi Minh of North Vietnam	1945–69	1.7 million
Pol Pot of Columbia	1975–79	1.7 million
Saddam Hussein of Iraq	1969–2003	2 million
Yahya Khan of Pakistan	1969–71	2 million
Hideki Tojo of Japan	1941–44	4 million
Vladimir Lenin of Russia	1917–24	6 million
Hirohito of Japan	1926–89	6 million
Chiang Kai-Shek of China	1928–49	10 million
Adolf Hitler of Germany	1934–45	20 million
Joseph Stalin of Russia	1941–53	23 million
Mao Zedong of China	1943–76	42.5 million

All these facts and figures are available on Google, and there are so many other names we can mention: Mr Idi Amin of Uganda, Colonel Gaddafi of Libya, American presidents involved in so many countries—there is no end to this list. Natural disasters should not worry you as much because nature always gives some kind of warning before it happens. You should watch out for our world politicians; you never know who is going to create doomsday and when.

You may not know there are a number of countries who have focused their nuclear missiles with a fixed range and target to destroy major cities of this world. If any person who is in charge in these places loses one's temper or gets depressed, it could be due to personal problems and can trigger the buttons. It is the disbelief of religious people that one day God is going to destroy this world. I can assure you that one day, we humans will make sure, this world is destroyed.

May you be with God, who is always with you.

———

ETERNAL YOUTH

I am sure this is one of the most favourite subjects of everyone in this world. We admire ourselves every morning by standing in front of the mirror. Some people do this all day, especially the people in the film industry or in modelling. People spend a fortune on beauty products or plastic surgery. Do you know all these practices push forward to age quicker, and many plastic surgeries have gone wrong? You have lost little bit of youth you had. This is why some people believe in ageing gracefully.

Many religions stress that you must remember you are going to die one day. They actually mean you should not commit any bad karma because after death, you are going to face the king of the dead, where all your wrong-doings will be counted for. Instead, people take it the other way: that you are going to die one day. These thoughts bring fear within, and this fear becomes the killer of your youth.

One of the best-known practices is to do regular physical exercise and pay attention to your diet. This way you can feel better and stay healthy most of your life, but age and family genes play their part too. Despite all your efforts, wrinkles begin to appear and hair turns grey; loss of hair is very common. I knew one saint named Baba Sadhu Singh; I did mention his name in my book *The Will of God*. He knew me since I was child, when I was about fourteen and he was fifty-two years old. At that time, all his beard was white or grey in colour.

The last time I saw him, in 2006, he was ninety-one years old. To my surprise, 90 percent of his beard had turned back to its original black colour. I have the photos to prove the before and after. During this meeting, we discussed it, and the conclusion was that as a saint, he has been in meditation most of his life. I noticed that he lost some body weight, but he made a remark that he hardly felt the need for physical food.

I have mentioned in our writings that in Agam-Des, where Sri Yabal Sakabi is the Master and is in-charge of this spiritual city, all the people working for him are called God-eaters (spiritual energy). It is the atmosphere within this spiritual city and the work they do. It is all related to Spirit. When doing this kind of work, you are dwelling in Spirit all the time. Spirit becomes your food intake instead of physical food; with this spiritual food, you do not age.

For example, if you are a youth of twenty-five years, you will remain the same forever as long as you are part of this spiritual city. This is why no one wants to leave, but everyone is not welcome to stay or join. Many visitors come to receive teachings, and at the end of the discourse they leave. All these visitors are also saints or soul travellers. This spiritual city is in the remote Hindu-Kush Mountains, near the border of Afghanistan and Kashmir. In these mountains, there are a number of spiritual places and bases for so many other saints.

Rebazar Ji is over 550 years old, and there are some who are older than him. These mountains are the origin of a number of rivers as well, and one of them is the Jhelum. At the head waters of this river, there is a spring of pure water known as Nirmala-Charan, the fountain of youth, or the waters of immortality. After drinking this water, any person can become immortal. Very few are aware of this, and for those saints who are based there, it is their secret for staying young forever. This spot is not very easy to find and is also guarded by Spirit.

Alexander the Great, was born in Pella, Greece in 356 BC and died very young at the age of thirty-two years in Babylon on 10 June 323 BC.

The cause of his death is still unknown. After conquering the empire of Persia, Alexander entered these mountains to wage a war against King Porus of Punjab (at present known as Pakistan). When Alexander reached this point, a spiritual saint appeared with Nirmala-Charan and offered for Alexander to drink it.

This saint could see the future and the killing of so many innocent people. His intention was if Alexander drank this water, his intentions of war would change, and he would become a spiritual at heart. Alexander was a king and did not trust this offering, taking it as some kind of deception. As he drew his sword to strike this saint, the man disappeared into thin air. The battle took place between King Porus, and Alexander won the war but became friend with King Porus.

He had the desire to conquer the whole world, but from there he returned to the west. This battle is also known as the Battle of River Jhelum. I think it was his destiny to reach India and fight. I also mentioned another saint, Baba Harnam Singh, in our Bhagty-Marg chapter in *The Way of God*. Once, he made up his mind to sit for lengthy meditation, which was at least one year in one go, without getting up to achieve any spiritual success.

The question is who was looking after his body and food? It was Spirit. When you are so dedicated, you become part of God's spiritual scheme, or you become a God-eater. You do not consume any physical food but Spirit within will provide for all relevant needs. You can live without any intake of physical food or drinking water. There is the pure spiritual fountain within. I do not have to prove this to anyone, but those people who are very close to me know that I've hardly eaten from the last four to five years.

Also, I did not drink clear water all my life. Sometimes I wonder why people drink so much water, and they say you cannot live without it. Yes, maybe. I do drink some tea or juice, but I never experienced what thirst or hunger is. All these foods and liquids are necessary to eat or drink. At the same time, people age as well, and so this cannot be the perfect food for us. Up to some extent, I have access to this spiritual food, and one time I thought of staying young forever like Rebazar Ji and many others.

It took me a few years to understand to not do it, and so I changed my mind. I felt that it is good to stay young and achieve longevity, but after many years when all known people pass away and new generations appear, then you become unknown to them and a stranger to everyone. Longevity is more a phenomenon to be created than pleasure. Then you will lose your interest to live any more in physical, unless you have been given some spiritual task like many other saints.

There are ways and means of maintaining eternal youth forever, but you have to adopt spiritual ways of living, or you can live for a very long life as you have become a spiritual saint. Then you can also leave your body at will and move into the eternal world of living. Eternal youth is only possible once you move out of mortal living. There is so much we can do, but we are so attached to this world that we forget to explore our true abilities. Whatever you can imagine, you can do because it already exists; otherwise you cannot imagine it.

May you live forever

IMPORTANCE OF LIVING

To acknowledge any achievement in this world, physical embodiment is very important. Otherwise, it does not exist as far as this world is concerned. I know there are so many spiritual beings who are working in invisible forms to keep balance of all universes, but no one knows that it is taking place. It is important for them to do this, but it is not acknowledged on the world level. All these presidents and prime ministers are thinking that they are running this world, but to the contrary, these unknown spiritual beings are sorting out the destruction created by our world political conflicts.

These spiritual corrections are never acknowledged because they cannot be recorded anywhere. This is why the importance of living is necessary if you want to make your mark in this world. How important is it to make your mark in this world? As far as I am concerned, not at all. Most extraordinary people don't want their work to be acknowledged because whatever they are doing is for them to know only. People around you notice what you do, and they talk about it because they are learning from what you provide.

Otherwise, this extraordinary knowledge is beyond their reach. This way, through these people you have left your mark in this world. It is very important to do something worthwhile; otherwise, thousands of children are born every day and thousands of people die every day, but no one knows who they are or were. Due to many known or unknown reasons, I am here and doing my spiritual endeavours but I do not wish to be acknowledged in any manner.

I cannot help writing what I know. God has given me the gift of spiritual knowledge, and in the sense, I feel my duty that others should know so they can benefit too. I do not approach anyone for this, but whoever somehow comes my way to learn what I know. I tell them it is their free will to apply spiritual principles in their lives. This way, what you know automatically becomes your mark in this world. Despite all this, it is my wish that at the end of my life span, people shouldn't know who I was.

But while I am still living, I am learning too. That is a plus point for my soul too because any journey made into the physical world is never wasted. Each journey made by any soul is very important because during each incarnation, we learn something, which is recorded in the files of our soul regarding what has taken place. Lower worlds are our training ground, and the soul has left its true home in the spiritual worlds to learn.

It's similar to how we leave our physical homes and walk to school every day for this purpose. All these academic qualifications are achieved only by leaving home. Very rarely can we achieve the same by sitting at home.

Lead your life as directed by God.

MY SPIRITUAL JOURNEY
BY SEEKER

The spiritual Master always says, "Truth is never denied if the Seeker is ready." I said many times: if the Seeker is serious on this spiritual path and is willing to listen and follow instructions from the Master, then a period of five years is far too long. The Seeker has been our member for just three years and has explored the kingdom of God up to the God-Realisation position. The whole experience took place in one night on 15 May 2018.

The Seeker took the teachings very seriously from day one and had lots of good karma from previous lives as well. There are eleven experiences in total. The Seeker had many other very uplifting spiritual experiences as well within last three years. Ten experiences took place in one night, and one prior experience relating to this realisation is shown in advance. The Seeker is physically awake at the beginning and ending of each experience, to acknowledge that what has taken place.

Each time the Seeker noted the time. During these experiences, the Master and Spirit take over the Seeker's spiritual journey. The Seeker has seen so much, but we have tried to use a minimum of words. I am sure this experience will encourage so many Seekers who want to see the glimpse of God's worlds. The Seeker wants to remain anonymous, and that is her free will, so instead we are going to use word Seeker.

The following are the Seeker's own words.

All these ten experiences took place in one night between 11 p.m. and 7 a.m., and I experienced the totality of spiritual worlds and its related knowledge. Above all, I saw all my past lives and future forecasts as well.

First Experience: Spiritual Masters, 11 p.m.

I was sitting with Krystal, my dog, because she was not feeling well. I was stroking her back and saying Satnam Ji (lord of the soul plane). Then suddenly an experience opened up, and all the world's religious Spiritual Masters or Gurus begin to appear before me one by one. It was a small screen before my eyes, and each Master appeared—not still as in a photograph but as if they were alive. Once I was satisfied with Darshan of any Master, then the next Master would appear on the same screen.

Darshan means the glimpse of a holy man. This Darshan of Masters begins with Sri Guru Nanak Dev of Sikhism, and then I was blessed by the Darshan of other nine gurus. These were the ten gurus of Sikhism, and then it was followed by Baba Nand Singh and Isher Singh Ji of Nanak Sar, and Baba Isher Singh Ji of Rarhe-wale. Then they were followed by all gurus of Hinduism, such as Sri Ram, Sri Krishna, Shiv Ji and Parvati, and Mahatma Buddha.

Then Sri Paul Ji, Darwin, Shams Mohd of Tabriji, Rebazar JI, Fubbi Kants, Yam-Raj, Yam-Dutes, Jesus Christ, Mohammad, and so many more world religious Masters were introduced by Sher Ji. I was told the name of each Master, but now I forgot them. I can clearly state I had the privilege of seeing all world spiritual Masters who ever existed. Once this Darshan came to an end, I came back to my normal state again, thanked Master Sher Ji, and said, "Shukria" thank you, Satnam Ji." Another experience opened up.

Second Experience: My Past Lives

Sher Ji asked me if I wanted to go in past and see my past lives. I was so glad to hear this and instantly, I said yes. In the majority of my past lives, I was a very beautiful and glamorous woman in different countries. I was a black woman too who was so beautiful, and later I was an English lady sitting in horse-driven carts. Next, I was shown that I was part of the Indian royal family (Shahi-Parivar), princess of one of the Riyasat "State" as well.

I saw myself in so many female forms or in female costumes in the majority of my past lives. I asked Sher Ji, "Have I been female all the time?"

He replied, "No. First you will see all important female-based past lives. Then I will show your male-based past lives." After this conversation, I was shown all my past lives as male. I saw myself living in different countries and holding different statuses in these lives, whether rich or poor and living in a hut. I lived in jungles and was also part of different religions according to the country I was living in at that time.

All souls go through this process of male or female forms while incarnated on the physical plane. In one of them, I was the manager (or responsible person) to look after the final resting place of Shiv Ji in India. After learning and seeing so much, I asked Sher Ji to pause for little while so I could write down what I had seen so far. Otherwise, I wouldn't be able to remember everything. Sher Ji replied in Punjabi, "Kaun Kambakhat Kehnda Hai ke Yaad Rakh? (Who fool asks you to remember all?)

What you saw so far is your past and gone." Sher Ji added, "Look ahead and carry on with your spiritual life. If you require any important information in the future from your past lives, it will be revealed to you in flashbacks." Looking at Sher Ji, I said, "I am grateful and thankful." Then I said, "Shukria" thank you to "Satnam Ji" and suddenly, another experience began. I remember very clearly saying to Sher Ji, "What you have shown me so far is more than enough for tonight. Now it is too late, and I want to go to sleep."

Sher Ji told me off and said in Punjabi, "Tu bahut Boldi hai, Tenu chup rehan di lorh hai. (You speak too much; you need to stay in silence.)" He also said to me, "Stay in silence for a few days so that I can stay in balance after seeing and knowing so much." Then Sher Ji added, "Today I want to give you lots of spiritual teachings, so do not interrupt me."

Third Experience: Journey

In this experience, Sher Ji and I were walking along the farmlands where wheat was grown. I started to walk on top of the bank of the small water Canal "Khaal", and I was slipping from this tapered bank time after time. I asked Sher Ji if I could walk in the middle of the canal water, which was used to provide water to boost the growth of wheat. This canal was empty or dry at that time. He said, "Yes, but stay in gunnia (balance)."

It was a very long walk, and then suddenly water began to flow in this canal. Gradually the water level rose. As we walked ahead, I saw lots of dry leaves and dry grass being collected, and a whirlpool appeared. I was standing in front of that whirlpool, and suddenly water came with lots of pressure. I fell on my back. My feet were pointing towards that whirlpool, and the next minute I felt that I had been pushed into that whirlpool.

I was sliding along the flow of high-speed water, and there were lots of bends in this canal. I faced the challenge at every bend, and many times my body did somersaults. The water was so cold and clean that it seemed ice had just melted. After enjoying my long ride above the water, my body was thrown into the melted golden ocean. My eyes opened, and I said, "Shukria" thank you, Satnam Ji." My next experience opened up.

Fourth Experience: Karma-less

I remember saying to myself, *I won't say, "Shukria, thank you, Satnam Ji," because every time I mention this word, Satnam Ji's experience begins.* I was trying to avoid any future experiences because I was so happy with what I'd seen so far. As soon as I mentioned the words again for not saying, "Shukria, Satnam Ji," I felt a sharp pain. I felt a sharp needle being poked in my left shoulder, and I said again, "I am not going to say Shukria."

Another sharp needle was poked in my left arm, and I said, "You can sew me with needles if you want to, Satnam Ji." After that, my whole body was poked with needles from all directions. I heard Sher Ji saying, "One more needle to go on top of your head. That is when the whole process will finish." Then I heard a very loud voice, and someone called Sher Ji by another name, a spiritual name. I saw a very big giant coming down from a very high place. He had a body like any body builder: big muscles, wide chest, and a bald head.

As he came down, Sher Ji had the last needle to poke in my head, and as soon as that needle went in my head, the big giant fell on top of me and entered my body. Then Sher Ji entered and disappeared in my body too. I heard that big giant asked Sher Ji if he could remove all the needles from my body. Then Sher Ji removed most of the needles, and when Sher Ji began to remove needles from my left arm, I stopped him by saying, "Please leave these few needles in my left arm so that I will stay connected with you."

Then I woke up and said, "Shukria" thank you, Satnam Ji." This big giant was Satnam Ji, and poking needles in the body is a symbol of defusing karma. Only karma-less people can enter into the soul plane, so Sher Ji was preparing my journey into the pure spiritual planes.

Leaving few needles in my arm is a symbol to indicate that my karma account is still open in this world till the end of my present life span.

Fifth Experience: Crossing the Lower Plane

Another experience started as soon as I said, "Satnam Ji." I was sitting on the edge of my bed "awake", and I saw Sher Ji walk into my room. I looked in his eyes, which were shining like spotlights. He had long, curly hair and did not utter a single word to me. He kept looking at me, and in the next minute I could see that Sher Ji turned into a big, shining star—and I was a star too. The big, shining star was going up and up very fast, and I followed the big star.

We as stars were going through so many different clouds, Green clouds, Pink clouds, Orange clouds, Blue clouds, Purple clouds. All different colours of clouds are a symbol of crossing each lower plane. We approached Golden clouds and then Sher Ji said to me, come quick and fast we need to crossover to the other side before the door closes. I can see there was a little pathway to follow and very narrow door. I saw the big shining star gone through and asked me to be very quick as the door was about to close.

I tried my best to go as fast as I could. I was in the middle of crossing that slim door, and it was closing. I got stuck in that door. It was so tight that I tried to pull myself out, and finally I managed to pull myself as a star. After that, I looked like a long, slim, shining star which had a tail. My tail got stuck in that tight door, and that was very painful. With pain I woke up physically. Sher Ji said, "We have to try again some other time."

My little tail stuck in that door is a symbol of indicating that a little more preparation is required, or it was reluctance on the part of the Seeker because the Seeker had already seen beyond her expectations.

Sixth Experience: Final Crossover

I was trying to go to sleep after having so many experiences in one night. I saw Sher Ji again in my room, and I remember saying to him, "You are back again, Sher Veer Ji "Brother" I cannot take any more teachings tonight because I am tired. And how will I remember all this? You don't even allow me time to write in my book."

Sher Ji said in Punjabi, "Kaun Kambakhat Kehnda Ke Yaad Rakh Sabh Kush. (What fool asks you to remember everything?) Everything will go in your subconscious mind, and each page will come out when required." (Harek panna jaddo jaroorat paie) in Punjabi. He was telling me off because I spoke a lot, and Sher Ji said, "I am going to make you stay in an aeroplane and strike you off on the way to Heathrow Airport, because you are speaking too much."

The next minute, I found myself turned into a model of an aeroplane. Sher Ji told me, "Go into the inner worlds and on the other side of the soul plane." I obeyed and started my journey, but the aeroplane was so heavy and had no flexibility in it. I found it very difficult to move that aeroplane through slim streets within high golden buildings. Then I told Sher Ji that I wanted to change my plans to reach the other side. Sher Ji said, "Yes, as you wish."

I thanked Sher Ji and said, "I will try again with my **guardian angel,** but not now, some other time." Sher Ji said, "It is up to you how quickly you want to do so. The longer you wait, the longer you have to bear the pain in your tail". I said, "OK, Sher Ji, we will go there very soon". I tried to sleep, and then Krystal, my dog, woke me up because she wanted to go outside as usual. I got out from my bed to take Krystal in the back garden.

Seventh Experience: 3.50 a.m.

I took Krystal out. It was very regular for her to wake me up at this time, between 3.30 and 4 a.m. After some time, I called Krystal to come back indoors. She was coming towards the kitchen door from the other end of garden, and as she reached the halfway point, I heard someone say to her, "Rukk, means stop." Krystal stopped and turned her face back, and she kept watching someone for a long time. I called her again to come back indoors. She came back, and I heard the words, "See you on the other side."

Sher Ji crept inside the house, and I said to him, "I can see you are back again."

He told me off and screamed at me, "Mai tere aaj Thappar Marna Hai. (I am going to slap you today.)"

I said to Sher Ji, "First you tell me who gave you the right to tell me off like this?"

He replied, "You yourself have given me this right. Do you remember the day you came for your initiation, and I asked you to bring five fruits with you? During initiation I explained to you that these five fruits were the symbol of submitting your five bodies—physical, astral, causal, mental, soul—to Spirit. Now I am in you, and you are in me." I bent down to him and touched his feet in respect for the first time. I went upstairs in my room, and I heard Sher Ji saying to me, "Try again with the guardian angel to go to the other end."

I said, "OK, Sher Ji."

Eighth Experience: Success

The **guardian angel** said, "Shall we go?" I said, "Yes, let us go."

The angel and I were flying so high in the sky and then so many beautiful cities and high buildings all of same colour, beautiful city with purple buildings and beautiful gardens with all the purple flowers and so-so many more. Purple colour is a symbol of being in Etheric or Sub-Conscious Plane. After a beautiful purple city, we went to the city of gold, and again there were beautiful high buildings. The angel was flying so high and so fast.

Then suddenly the guardian angel started to fly even faster and asked me to hold on to her tightly. The angel said, "We have to reach other end before the door shuts." The door was about to close. Then the angel kept flying like a big bird through narrow streets and high buildings. We saw a little door, and the angel and I both smiled as she said, "We are nearly there." We could see the door, which we have to cross to go to the other side of the soul plane.

The angel said, "Hold on to me very tight." We both wanted to reach the other side, and the angel jumped through that door as it was closing. We managed to go through that door, and the angel said, "We have done it." Upon reaching the other side of that door, what I saw a big gold brick in front of my eyes, sitting on the tip of my nose. This gold brick was shining so brightly that I could not see anything, I asked Sher Ji, "What is this?"

He said, "Keep on walking." I obeyed him and continued.

That gold brick started moving slowly to my right side. I saw a very muddy, slim walkway which was very curly, I kept walking, and that turned into a straight path with golden bricks laid in a beautiful design. Then I noticed there was a milestone on my left, and it was made of gold too. As I kept walking, a few more milestones came. On the last one, there were some numbers, 41788, indicating many more milestones to my final destination.

As our journey continued, far away I saw another very big white milestone. On this milestone letters were written in a vertical manner. Vertical is also a symbol of travelling to the higher planes. I tried to read, but it was difficult because we were moving along. I tried once more and managed to read only first three letters: ANA ... Anami-Lok is the tenth spiritual plane. If we add up all these numbers, or milestones, it is $4 + 1 + 7 + 8 + 8 = 28$.

If we further add up, then 28 is $2 + 8 = 10$, and that also indicates your final destination is Anami-Lok. It is totally unbelievable how accurate Spirit is when showing all these symbols to us. All we need is a little effort to unveil the mystery of the symbol and understand the actual meaning of the experience taking place. As the experience continued, anything in our vision was pure white or silver. White or silver are symbols of higher planes above the soul plane.

Sat-Lok's colour is gold, Alakh-Lok's is light gold, and Alaya-Lok's is a fading gold colour. Hakikat-lok, Agam-lok, and Anami-lok are pure white or silver. The destination to Anami-Lok was reached. As soon as this experience finished, I woke up and said, "Shukria" thank you, Satnam Ji," and another experience opened.

> It seems to me that "Shukria, Satnam Ji" are
> my magic words to the secret worlds.

Ninth Experience: Celebration

The night of 15 May was my blessed night because I had so many experiences. Again, Sher Ji came in my room with another seven Masters. I was so glad and happy, and I did not know what to say or do. Then we all ate Besan Ladoos (an Indian sweet) to celebrate my spiritual journey. As the Masters were leaving, they blessed me too. Sher Ji said, "Now I am going as well."

I asked him, "Is there any message for me?"

He said, "You are a naked soul," and he opened my front door to leave. Upon asking, Sher Ji explained to me, "Naked soul means you are karma-less; otherwise you would not be travelling this far." I thanked

God and said, "Shukria, Satnam Ji," and instantly another experience started.

Tenth Experience: Future

Sher Ji came back and said, "I am going to show you your future."

I said, "What did you say, Sher Ji?"

He said, "You heard me correct." He showed me my future and said to me, "Now write your future in your own words, in the shape of a manuscript, You will not remember what you have just seen, but once any important situations or happenings take place in your life, then you will see the same situation in flashbacks." At the end of this experience, I came back to my normal senses, and I noted the time: 7 a.m.

During the second experience, I saw all my past lives, and in this experience, I have been revealed the future. To know your future is good, but at the same time knowing a few situations up front could be disturbing because they may not be in your favour. This is the story of each individual, and on that basis, God draws a curtain over our past lives and futures.

I was told by Sher Ji that in the future when any important situation takes place, there and then I will get the flashback, and knowingness will come to indicate that this was shown to me earlier. Since that day, a few important situations have occurred in my life, and instantly I saw the flashback of acknowledging the information received earlier. This is exactly what happened in the past history of Hinduism.

Saint Valmiki wrote Ramayana before the story of Ramayana was completed in real life. So, this chapter is going to be my Ramayana, and it is going to reveal my future because it will unfold or take shape in my life. In the beginning or end of each experience, I was fully awake physically and noted the time on the clock. During the experiences, it was spiritual Master Sher Ji teaching, and my soul was learning.

I am blessed by Spirit, Sher Ji, and Satnam Ji. According to my eighth experience, we added up all numbers (41788), and the answer came as 10, which was our symbol for Anami-Lok. Now, if we add up 10 in the same manner (1 + 0), the answer is 1. There is only one God, so I am blessed by God too. May the blessings be.

The Seeker

15 May 2018

To the Seeker: you have seen the truth. Now you are the Master of your own universe.

Sher Gill

MY UNIVERSE

It is misfortune for this world because most of the countries and religions are divided so badly that each wants to be better, stronger, and more powerful than others. Some are silent, and a majority of them declare openly to be enemies to this or that country or religion. Each is power hungry and tries to outsmart the others. They all want to dominate, but whom? To the whole world, in effect they are deceiving themselves. What is this wholeness?

They will never understand that we are incomplete without the others—not by power but without their love. It is the love of this universe that makes you complete. There are a million miles of gap between us as being humans. Do you know why? Religions are the main cause. We believe our religions are leading us to God, but they are only adding oil to the fire. All these religious scholars are so busy that they have forgotten God and accepted politics as their goal.

Most of their time and energy is wasted on how to complete a number of four- or five-year terms. From this you can draw conclusions. Are they interested in you, or are they keen on self-service? This is not limited to them only. This power is passed over in families for generations. I can name a number of these families in India and Pakistan. Their present generations are not capable of leading their nations, but full force is being used to make them the faces of their nations.

All these ministers and presidents promise to serve their countries, but most of their energy is used to overload their own bank accounts. What can these nations gain under this kind of leadership? It is disgrace and unfortunate for these countries. That is why these countries are called Third World countries. God created this world to look like heaven, and all humans are created equal and very close to its heart. But these power-hungry people call themselves kings, queens, and ministers while the majority of the public is called labourers, slaves, or low caste.

In the eyes of God, there is no caste, no rich or poor—just princes and princesses of God and heirs to the throne. Religious saints and astrologers threaten this world a number of times and threaten their followers that on a certain day, God is going to destroy this world. None of their forecasts have come true, and do you know why? They are all fake gurus and misusing people's invested trust. Hinduism, Islam, Christianity, and all major religions are the backbone of politics.

Where is God? Who is God? That is totally forgotten. All these nuclear-minded people will destroy this world, but not God. There is no value for humans or God's creation. History keeps repeating itself every few years. You will notice that most of the powerful people received some kind of prophecy by some live oracles, saints, or astrologers, to the effect that they are born to rule this world. Once this belief imprints in their minds, then naturally all their actions are driven to execute this prophecy; the cost or loss is never considered.

Here you will notice at the end of the day, all these oracles, saints, and astrologers are responsible for many destructions. This was part of Alexander's belief and many others. In the early days, Alexander the Great was one man and wished to rule all as the most powerful person in this world. After his father, King Phillip, died by assassination, it is believed he was the son of Zeus, who was considered the ruler of the Olympian gods in Greece.

His mother claimed one day before her wedding that the spiritual light of Zeus struck into her womb, and she felt the pregnancy. Alexander killed every man who stood in his path of power. His journey begins from Macedonia to the Persian Empire and finally to India. During his journey of invasion to other countries, at least one million people died. This was a very high number of deaths considering there were fewer people at that time.

In World War I, the total number of casualties accounted for were 41 million, comprising of 11 million military personnel, 7 million civilians died, and 23 million wounded.

In World War II, the total number of casualties are unknown, but over 60 million people died. About 20 million military personnel and 40 million civilians died due to bombing, massacres, starvation, diseases, and deliberate genocide. About 1.3 million British military personnel died in this war.

In the Napoleonic war, the battlefields toured Egypt, Belgium, Holland, Italy, Austria, Germany, Poland, Spain, and most of Europe. Can you imagine the number of people dead or wounded? If you go through world history and see how many major wars or conflicts took place, and how many people died, you will be speechless. Now, are we still blaming God for this?

At present, some countries are ready to repeat this history if they get the opportunity. Now, can someone tell me what God has to do with this? You know all these fake saints and astrologers who are pulling some cheap stunts by saying that God is going to destroy this or that. God is the creator of all universes, not the destroyer. Humans are always responsible for their own destruction for a number of reasons.

The whole world is divided. Forget about the nations—with the help of Kal, there is a mini Government within each family. There is hardly evidence of Godly love, and domination over others is more important.

I wish everyone could think, act, or believe like I do. I am part of the whole universe. I do not believe in any religion or any particular country. The whole universe in mine, and destruction can only stop when we act as one.

When you are a universal being, it is so satisfying and peaceful. Being part of only one country or nation or religion is very irritating because you have no tolerance for others. We are all pilgrims here to do spiritual learning and die naturally. Regarding the land you claimed to be yours in deed papers, after your death, someone else's name will appear on the papers. It is the same land and will remain the same; only the ownership names change, and there is nothing you can do about it.

This world is created as a whole. This whole land is joined together as one piece on the surface or under the sea. All five oceans are one too. All these religions are man-made. It is the weakness of humans to follow one for many purposes, to create self-identity, and to socialise with each other. All religions have become part of politics, and so they fail to give spiritual succour to their followers. To socialise is good for occupying the mind, but it is also responsible for self-created problems.

People are more interested in sorting out self-created problems than God. This is why God is beyond their reach. Neither are people interested in God; the majority of their time is spent with thoughts on money, status in society, and the luxuries of this world. One day they will have the realisation that God is waiting for them with open arms.

May the truth be yours.

—

SILENT LEGENDS

There are thousands of silent legends in this world, but we cannot mention their names because they always remain anonymous. At the same time, we cannot write much on this subject for the same reason. Many people live in remote places, or they make sure their identities remain hidden. You will notice the majority of them are shy in nature. They are not working for name or fame. Many people don't realise something done silently is a lot more pleasing and satisfying than big bangs.

They have all the abilities as any living or dead legend, but they are the people who are in the background, the champion makers. We know thousands of living legends at present. People appreciate what they do, but they do not realise, there is always someone in the background who is the backbone of others' success. We never bothered to know because we are so busy admiring the current champions. All the Olympic gold medal winners have coaches; if they did not coach the athletes properly, their achievements would be a lot less.

At the same time, all these coaches have setbacks too. Maybe when they were young, they had the ability, but due to a lack of coaching or facilities, they missed their mark. Now they want to make sure you, as their student, can achieve what they could not. This way they feel satisfied too. Many saints have their gurus who have shown the way towards enlightenment. Without their spark, you would have been nothing, but they remain anonymous.

We know the names of the first three people who landed on the moon in 1969, but we never know how many people worked in the background to accomplish their mission. We know the legends, but the makers of legends are always unknown. That is why I call them silent legends, and I felt like writing a few words to show our appreciation.

I am a very simple man, but to make me who I am and to provide me with what I know, there was the effort of so many spiritual people. Without their help, I would not know as much or be as successful. Above all, God, Satnam Ji, and Sri Paul Ji made sure that I was spiritually trained. **God is behind every legend ever created,**

But it is Silent.

Good Readings to you

Sher Gill

Printed in the United States
By Bookmasters